Men-at-Arms • 480

Napoleon's Dragoons of the Imperial Guard

Ronald Pawly • Illustrated by Patrice Courcelle

Series editor Martin Windrow

First published in Great Britain in 2012 by Osprey Publishing,
Midland House, West Way, Botley, Oxford, OX2 0PH, UK
44-02 23rd Street, Suite 219, Long Island City, NY 11101, USA
E-mail: info@ospreypublishing.com

OSPREY PUBLISHING IS PART OF THE OSPREY GROUP

A CIP catalogue record for this book is available from the British Library

Print ISBN: 978 1 84908806 0
PDF ebook ISBN: 978 1 84908 807 7
ePub ebook ISBN: 978 1 78096 404 1

Editor: Martin Windrow
Page layout by: Melissa Orrom Swan, Oxford
Index by Alan Thatcher
Typeset in Helvetica Neue and ITC New Baskerville
Originated by PDQ Media, Bungay, UK
Printed in China through Worldprint Ltd.

12 13 14 15 16   10 9 8 7 6 5 4 3 2 1

Osprey Publishing is supporting the Woodland Trust, the UK's leading
woodland conservation charity, by funding the dedication of trees.

www.ospreypublishing.com

Author's Note

Readers should note that this and the author's other relevant titles listed below
represent, collectively, a nearly comprehensive digest drawn from the
regimental archives of the Cavalry of the Guard. To avoid wasteful duplication,
some material relating to the Guard Cavalry as a whole – organization,
strengths, movements, etc – is not repeated, so readers will find it worthwhile
to cross-reference between this book and MAA 378, 389, 429, 433, 440, 444
and 456. They may also find Elites 115 and 116, on *Napoleon's Imperial
Headquarters*, useful in this context.

Artist's Note

Readers may care to note that the original paintings from which the colour
plates in this book were prepared are available for private sale. All reproduction
copyright whatsoever is retained by the Publishers. All enquiries should be
addressed to:

Patrice Courcelle, 33 avenue de Vallons, 1410 Waterloo, Belgium

The Publishers regret that they can enter into no correspondence upon this
matter

NAPOLEON'S DRAGOONS OF THE IMPERIAL GUARD

THE EMPRESS'S DRAGOONS

An officer of the Dragoons of the Guard, after Martinet, emphasizing the elegant appearance of the helmet and uniform. The horses were to be chestnut, though each squadron probably favoured its own exact shade. The regimental barracks in Paris were at the Caserne des Carmelites in the Rue de Grenelle. (© Collection & photo Bertrand Malvaux, France)

In spite of historical evidence to the contrary, popular legend has it that every 30 May, on the anniversary of the death of the Empress Josephine in 1814, former courtiers and officers of Napoleon's Imperial Guard would gather at the little village church of St Pierre-St Paul in Rueil, close to the Malmaison estate that had once been her residence, to commemorate her passing. Some of those who attended wore dark green uniforms with white lapels and magnificent Grecian-style brass helmets, identifying them as officers of the Dragoons of the Imperial Guard – better known as the Empress's Dragoons.

1806: Creation and establishment

By 1806, following the triumph of Austerlitz, the Imperial Guard was still a modest force made up almost entirely of veterans of the Consular Guard, who had seen action during the early campaigns in Italy, Egypt and lately in Germany. It consisted of a general staff; two regiments of infantry (Grenadiers and Chasseurs); two regiments of cavalry (Mounted Grenadiers and Mounted Chasseurs); an artillery regiment; a Legion of Gendarmerie d'Élite; a battalion of Sailors; one company of Mamelukes, and a company of Veterans. In addition, two battalions and one squadron of Vélites served with the infantry and cavalry respectively; these were young volunteers from wealthy families, who paid to serve as probationers in the hope of promotion.

It was presumably the contribution of the Line dragoons to the 1805 campaign that persuaded the emperor, by a decree of 15 April 1806, to honour them with representation in his Imperial Guard (there was already a dragoon regiment in his Italian Royal Guard). The Dragoons of the Guard would be organized on the same basis as the Mounted Grenadiers and Chasseurs, with a regimental staff, four squadrons of two companies each, plus a squadron of Vélites. The staff comprised the colonel, 2 majors (note that this was not a rank, but an appointment), 2 *chefs d'escadron* (squadron-leaders) of whom one served with the Vélites, 1 squadron-leader instructor, 1 *quartier-maître trésorier* (paymaster), 1 captain instructor, 2 adjutant-majors (one of them serving with the Vélites), 5 sub-adjutant-majors (of whom one with the Vélites), 4 standard-bearers, and 3 adjutant sub-lieutenants (responsible for *vivres*, rations; *fourrages*, forage and fodder; and *habillement*, clothing and personal equipment). There were 5 medical officers (2 first class and 3 second or third class); 1 instructor, and 1 *vaguemestre* (wagon-master), both with the rank of sergeant-major; 2 veterinary officers (of whom one with the Vélites) and 4 assistant veterinaries; 1 trumpet-major, 3 trumpet-corporals (of whom one with the Vélites) and 1 kettle-drummer; 2 master-farriers, and 6 master-craftsmen.

Each company had 1 captain, 1 first lieutenant, 2 second lieutenants, 1 sergeant-major, 8 sergeants, one quartermaster, 10 corporals, 96 dragoons, 3 trumpeters and 2 farriers. The Vélites were organized in two companies of 125 men each, exclusive of officers and NCOs, the latter being found from within the Mounted Grenadiers and Chasseurs. Before the decree of 15 April 1806 the Vélite cavalry squadrons of the Guard had been composed of four companies instead of the usual two; now each was reduced to two, so that the surplus of men could be transferred to the Dragoons.

Napoleon chose as the colonel of the regiment one of his Corsican cousins, the 28-year-old Jean Thomas Arrighi de Casanova. Arrighi had served in the army since 1796; he had distinguished himself in Egypt, at Marengo, and again during the Austerlitz campaign.

The troopers of the new regiment were to come from the 30 Line regiments of dragoons, and it was intended to form the first two squadrons by the end of 1806; each regiment was required to provide 12 dragoons with at least ten years of active service, but the NCOs and corporals were to come from the existing Guard Cavalry units. The emperor personally commissioned the officers, some from the Guard Cavalry and the rest from Line units; each dragoon regiment had to propose two lieutenants, from whom one would be chosen. The other two squadrons were to be organized in 1807, when each Line dragoon unit would have to provide another ten men.

Organization started on 1 July 1806, and the regimental staff was the first to reach completion. On 1 August the regiment numbered 7 officers, 249 rankers and 37 Vélites; another 781 officers and men, plus 274 Vélites, were needed to fill the establishment. The regiment in fact had more horses than men, so that Col Arrighi had to employ grooms to look after the surplus.

Officer, by Nicolas Hoffmann, 1806. Here the style of the helmet appears more 'Ancien Régime' – Hoffmann was already working before the Revolution, so would be familiar with this style. Less explicable are the eagle fitting instead of the usual *porte-aigrette* at the top front of the crest; the red-tipped green plume, instead of all red; the silver braid, instead of gold, on the holster covers; and the cuirassier-style sabre. (Anne S.K. Brown Military Collection, Brown University, Providence, USA)

* * *

In 1806 much of continental Europe was in Napoleon's power, but Prussia was aggressively anti-French. That summer Napoleon sent his Imperial Guard marching towards the Rhine, where they arrived by the end of September.

The emperor rejected a Prussian ultimatum demanding the withdrawal of all French troops stationed in Germany; Prussia invaded his ally Saxony, but its army was slow-moving. Napoleon's troops marched at such a speed that even the Guard had difficulty keeping up with the emperor. On 14 October 1806, in the separate battles of Jena and Auerstädt, Napoleon and Marshal Davout beat the Prussians decisively, and drove them back in a relentless pursuit. Within days, surrounded by his Guard, Napoleon entered Berlin in triumph, and his occupation of Prussia forced King Frederick William III to the negotiating table. Most Prussian troops capitulated, and on 16 November an armistice was signed at Charlottenburg; but this was not ratified by the king, for fear it would force him into war against Russia. Russian forces under Gen Bennigsen arrived on the Vistula river, and the Grande Armée advanced to face them.

Composite uniform of an officer in the former Brunon Collection. The only part identified to an owner is the helmet of *Chef d'escadrons* Chatry de Lafosse (see page 21). The coatee corresponds with those worn after 1809. The gilt brass buttons are of Guard pattern, bearing a crowned eagle. Those on the lapels, cuff patches, and securing the epaulettes measure 17mm; those on the rear waist and false pockets, and the three below the right lapel, are 26mm. The white waistcoat, with a 65mm-high collar, is fastened with eight small flat buttons. (Musée de l'Empéri, Salon de Provence)

1807: DEFINITIVE ORGANIZATION

These dramatic developments did not prevent Napoleon taking a continuing interest in the organization of his new Guard regiment. On 13 November, Gen Junot, Governor of Paris, had already sent 9 officers and 200 dragoons to join the army in the field. In a letter of the 30th the emperor told him that their horses were awaiting them in Berlin, but it was important that they brought their saddles with them; another 140 men who were now ready to be sent off would find their horses at Nancy (see also commentary, Plate E5). Napoleon wanted the regiment to have three squadrons in January 1807; Junot was instructed to send other men as soon as they were available, to make up the fourth squadron.

Bennigsen's Russian troops evacuated Warsaw to retire behind the Narew river; on 28 November, Marshal Murat and his troops entered the Polish capital, and three weeks later Napoleon arrived in person. On 13 January 1807, he asked Gen Clarke, Governor of Berlin, whether the Guard Dragoons had arrived there; two weeks later the emperor demanded, in rapid succession, when they would receive their horses, when the last detachment of 250 men would arrive, and when the regiment would become operational.

Early in 1807 the Russians suddenly advanced on Marshal Ney's corps. On 25 January, while Marshal Bernadotte was heading south in an attempt to stay in contact with Ney and the rest of the Grande Armée, at Mohrungen he ran into, and pushed aside, 10,000 Russians under Gen Markov. Two days later, Napoleon gave his orders for an advance towards the Russians in three strong columns. This forced the Russians to retreat towards their base at Königsberg; the pursuit was a continuous series of skirmishes, during which, on 5 February, Maj Fiteau of the Guard Dragoons was wounded.

Eylau and Friedland

On 7 February 1807 the two armies met near the village of Eylau, where an appalling, costly, but inconclusive battle in the snow took place the next day; it ended in a French victory simply in the sense that the Russians retreated and left them in possession of the battlefield. In a letter to Gen Duroc, Napoleon wrote: 'There was a particularly bloody battle yesterday at Preussich-Eylau. The battlefield was ours in the end, but the fact is both sides lost many men, and the distance makes my losses all the more crucial. Corbineau was taken by a cannonball; Marshal Augereau was lightly wounded; d'Hautpoul, Heudelet, and four or five other generals were wounded'. The Grande Armée soon went into winter quarters around Osterode, while the Russians retreated once again towards Königsberg.

On 6 March, Napoleon ordered Clarke to send all the Imperial Guard depots forward to Warsaw. He asked again when the Guard Dragoons

Dragoon in *tenue de ville*, after Martinet; compare with Plate E2. The full-dress coatee was worn with a bicorne hat and (officially) the deerskin breeches, but normally the latter were replaced with dark green wool or pale nankeen equivalents, depending upon the season. (© Collection & photo Bertrand Malvaux, France)

Strength on 1 January 1807: 30 officers and 393 rankers.
During 1806 the regiment had received 30 officers and 440 men from other corps, and 16 men entered as recruits. 24 troopers went to the Mounted Chasseurs of the Guard, 27 to the Mounted Grenadiers, 9 were returned to their former regiments, 1 died, and 2 were stricken from the rolls.

would join him, and requested a detailed report on the regiment's condition. Again, on 23 March he wrote impatiently to Clarke: 'You must have by now at least 200 mounted Dragoons of the Guard; let them march off for the army'.

In May, Napoleon ordered a renewed advance; but the Russians had already left their winter quarters, and attacked Marshal Ney's corps. Napoleon's countermove obliged Bennigsen to retreat to Friedland, where Marshal Lannes held them until Napoleon arrived with reinforcements. On 14 June the Russians were once again beaten with heavy losses, and fell back to the River Niemen. The Tsar asked for a truce, resulting in the peace treaty signed at Tilsit on 9 July between Napoleon, the Tsar and the King of Prussia, which imposed humiliating terms on both the allied sovereigns. During the battle of Friedland the Guard Dragoons stood on the left of the Guard Cavalry formation. Some sources state that two squadrons were present, with some 285 men in total. One of the casualties was Capt Adj-Maj Jolly, who was wounded (some of his paintings are reproduced in this book). In June, Col Arrighi was commissioned *général de brigade*, retaining his command of the Guard Dragoons (all regimental colonels of Guard units were general officers).

Trooper, 1809 or later, after Martinet. Note the double borders in *aurore* braid on the triple holster covers, rectangular-section portmanteau, and shabraque, the latter with the Imperial crown in the corner.
(© Collection & photo Bertrand Malvaux, France)

Reinforcing the Cavalry of the Guard

After three years of campaigning, the Guard Cavalry needed strengthening. On 8 July 1807, Napoleon decreed that the Line cavalry regiments were to provide 750 men, of which 400 were for the Dragoons; each Line dragoon regiment had to provide 11 men. All of them were to be found among those who had distinguished themselves at the battles of Austerlitz and Jena and those who had served during the latest campaign, and were to be veterans with at least four years' service (instead of the ten years' normally required).

On 1 August 1807 the Guard Dragoons' depot in Paris recorded 8 officers and 70 men, of whom 2 in hospital – this including 3 officers and 58 men from the Vélites. Serving with the army in the field were another 21 officers, 333 rankers and 8 Vélites; this gave a total of 29 officers and 403 men, plus 66 Vélites commanded by SqnLdr Rossignol. A month later, on 10 September, they mustered in total 46 officers and 640 rankers, of whom 1 was absent and 26 in hospital.

On 23 October, Napoleon disbanded the Gendarmes d'Ordonnance, a Guard corps recently created with volunteers from French noble families. The officers could choose whether to take their leave or continue to serve: the men who had served in the 1807 Polish campaign were assigned to other Guard Cavalry units, and 59 were incorporated in the Dragoons. In November, the Dragoons' depot reported 15 officers with 32 men, of whom 1 in hospital, plus, for the Vélites, 2 officers with 43 men, including 1 in hospital. With the army there were 47 officers with 624 men, plus 1 officer with 20 men from the Vélites. In all, the regimental strength was thus 718 Dragoons and 66 Vélites – a shortfall of 319 Dragoons and 246 Vélites. The documents also indicate that over a period of one month the regiment received 33 officers and 304 men, mainly coming from Line units.

Celebrating victory, preparing for war
With the emperor back in Paris, he summoned his Imperial Guard to the capital. (Although no expense would be spared on their welcome, and they would be greeted as the heroes of the hour, they were not allowed new uniforms to replace the ones in which they had campaigned.) After a night spent in the suburbs of Paris, at 1pm on 25 November 1807 they entered the city through the Porte Saint-Michel, marching via Rue de Rivoli to the Place du Carrousel and the Tuileries Palace, where they would lodge their regimental banners in the emperor's study (with the exception of the Dragoons, who had not yet received theirs). On 26 November the city gave a banquet for the Guard on the Champs-Elysées. The next day Marshal Bessières offered dinner to all the Guard's officers and the members of the capital's municipal government, and on the 30th he gave a ball with fireworks in honour of the Guard.

Napoleon, meanwhile, was already plotting his next foreign adventure, to bring under his control the political and military situation beyond the Pyrenees. While most continental European countries were under his control or influence, Portugal was alone in failing to fall into line with his 'Continental System', the decree forbidding trade with Britain. Spain's unpopular alliance with France had already cost it dearly; but the disunited royal family and government had been neutered by French manipulation, and no immediate barrier stood in the way of Napoleon's plan to punish the Portuguese. He gathered at Bayonne the Corps d'Observation de la Gironde, a 20,000-strong force commanded by Gen Junot. This corps obtained free passage through Spain, and crossed the Franco-Spanish border on 18 October 1807. On 30 November, and now renamed the Army of Portugal, they entered Lisbon with little resistance.

On 16 October, recognizing the inability of the Spanish government to control the anti-French sentiment among its population, the emperor had written to his minister of war that he intended to create a 2nd Corps of Observation of the Gironde near Bordeaux. With 30,000 men, of which 5,000 were cavalry, Gen Dupont's task would be to protect the supply lines of Junot's army and to support it when needed. Until then no Guard units had been committed, but on 16 November the emperor ordered the Guard Train battalion and a Guard Artillery officer to join Dupont's corps.

At about this time the Guard Dragoons were finally organized in four squadrons with a strength of 619 men present; of these, 500 men were ready to march off, and within a month they would increase to 600, without counting those 150 who were already at Bordeaux. New clothing, horses, saddles and harness were provided for 50 per cent of the dragoons, but the continuous need to send men forwards to the army complicated the task of organizing and equipping the regiment. Their young colonel, energetic and headstrong, was determined to make it one of the finest and most modern regiments in the Guard, and Napoleon approved his innovations in their uniforms. During one of the parades in Paris the Empress Josephine was struck by the elegant appearance of the new regiment, and she became their patroness; thereafter they proudly carried the unofficial title of 'the Empress's Dragoons'.

By now the opening of the border to Junot's army – and the demands of feeding it – were causing increasing unrest in Spain. On 13 November, Napoleon instructed Gen Clarke (now minister of war) that Gen Dupont's corps was to cross the border on the 22nd at the latest. Less than a month later, he instructed the minister to assemble more troops near the western end of the border, organized in a division under Gen Merle.

1808: SPAIN

Initial advances and setbacks

On 9 January, Marshal Moncey's Corps d'Observation de l'Océan marched into the province of Biscay heading for Vittoria via Burgos, and on the eastern flank Gen Duhesme's Division d'Observation des Pyrénées Orientales (Eastern Pyrenees) entered Catalonia and advanced towards Barcelona. At first everything went well enough – too well, in fact, for operations in a country of which Gen Beurnonville wrote: 'There are no roads, no transport, no houses, no stores nor provisions, in a land where the people warm themselves by means of the sun and can live on nothing; they are brave, audacious, proud, and the perfect assassins. They cannot be compared with other people – they like only themselves and love only God, whom they serve very badly.'

The concentration of the Guard regiments was kept secret, as it might be a sign that the emperor would lead them into Spain in person. On 1 February, the Dragoons had 14 officers with 183 men serving with the army in the South, and, step by step, more Guard units found their way towards Bayonne. On 18 February, Bessières was instructed to send large Guard detachments from Paris via Poitiers, and Gen Lepic, who was commanding the Guard elements at Bordeaux, was also instructed to march towards Bayonne, to arrive between 1 and 3 March at the latest. The Grand Marshal of the Palace, Duroc, was ordered to have the emperor's horses, coaches and wagons follow the troops leaving Paris for Bayonne.

With French troops now in Madrid, and Portugal controlled by Junot, three French columns marched deeper into Spain: Dupont's divisions via Valladolid towards Cadiz, to relieve the blockaded fleet; Marshal Moncey's, from Madrid towards Aranda; and Gen Duhesme's, still advancing on Barcelona. The chief command was given to Marshal Murat, with the title of Lieutenant of the Emperor in Spain. Crossing the Spanish border on 10 March, he found Gen Lepic with a 6,000-strong force of the Imperial Guard in Vittoria, and a part of these would follow him to Madrid. On the other side of the Pyrenees, Marshal Bessières was in command, from 19 March, of a Division d'Observation des Pyrénées Occidentales (Western Pyrenees), and was awaiting instructions.

A valuable colour drawing made during his service with the regiment (September 1806–August 1809) by *Capitaine adjutant-major*, later *Colonel* Louis Jolly. The accoutrements are those of a ranker, but the elegance of the subject suggests a *Vélite* in a uniform of officer quality; no *aurore* features are evident in the drawing. (Anne S.K. Brown Military Collection, Brown University, Providence, USA)

Detail of the left lapel of the Brunon Collection composite officer's uniform, woven from very fine white woollen material. The cross of the Legion of Honour is of the 1810 model. (Musée de l'Empéri, Salon de Provence)

When the Spanish royal family were spirited away to France and forced to renounce their throne, on 2 May a furious uprising began in Madrid, and was ruthlessly crushed by Murat. When Napoleon presented the Spanish crown to his brother Joseph, Murat was given the latter's former kingdom of Naples, in consolation for his own disappointed hopes. However, Spain was soon ablaze with armed resistance, mounted by regional commanders of the regular army supported by spontaneous civilian uprisings. On 14 July 1808, Bessières, having crossed the border, decisively defeated the Spanish Gen Joachim Blake's Army of Galicia at Medina de Rioseco. Bessières had some Guard units with him, among them Dragoons, who charged to relieve a company of voltigeurs of the 4th Light Infantry when they advanced too far. The regiment's casualties included SqnLdr Grandjean, 1st Lt Meyronnet and 2nd Lt Pisler.

Bessières's victory allowed King Joseph to enter Madrid on 20 July 1808, but not for long. On the 23rd, Gen Dupont, far to the south, was shockingly outmanoeuvred and forced to surrender to Gen Castanos's Army of Andalusia at Baylen. This victory astonished Europe, and encouraged Spanish resistance; after only ten days in his new capital Joseph fled Madrid, and all French troops retired northwards to the River Ebro.

Napoleon ordered Gen Walther to leave Paris for Bayonne with the larger part of the Guard that was still stationed in the capital. (When Guard units went on campaign, each was administratively divided into two *régiments de marche*; Walther was to leave in Paris the '2nd Regiments' of the Mounted Chasseurs, Mounted Grenadiers and Dragoons.) Walther's cavalry had to be in Bayonne on 30 October; when he arrived at his destination he found a letter from Napoleon telling him that Gen Lefèbvre-Desnoëttes was to leave Paris with the remainder of the Guard, and that Walther was to march into Spain.

Throughout these months, however, the Guard Dragoons were still struggling to get their numbers up. On 3 May 1808, Gen Clarke had included in a report marked 'very urgent' the following proposals. The regiment lacked 343 experienced soldiers and 208 Vélites. To meet Napoleon's wish to complete the regiment's numbers, Clarke suggested that the *departements* would provide the necessary Vélites. He and Gen Arrighi agreed that the best place to find the necessary experienced men was in the 23 Line dragoon regiments serving with the Grande Armée, and the 9th Regiment that was then marching towards Paris. (No men

Strength on 1 January 1808: 67 officers and 757 rankers.
During 1807 the regiment had received 37 officers and 379 men from other corps, and 34 entered as recruits. 15 troopers had returned to their former regiments, 1 went to the Military School at Fontainebleau, 10 were commissioned officers in the regiment, 1 went to the Veterans, 11 died, and 11 were stricken from the rolls.

would be demanded from the dragoons serving in Italy: it would take too long for them to reach Paris, and in any case such units would be unable to comply with the stipulation of 8 July 1807 that the men had to be veterans of Austerlitz, Jena and later battles.) Therefore the minister and the colonel suggested that six dragoon regiments with the Grande Armée (1st, 2nd, 4th, 14th, 20th and 26th) should provide 15 men each, for a total of 90. Seventeen regiments (3rd, 5th, 6th, 8th, 10th–13th, 15th–19th, 21st, 22nd, 25th and 27th) would provide 14 men each, totalling 238; and the 9th Dragoons would give

another 15 men. This would bring the grand total to the necessary 343 men. Those serving with the Grande Armée would be assembled in Berlin, travelling from there by coach to Mainz and thence to Paris. (In the event, more than one soldier chosen to serve in the Dragoons was too tall or too heavy for this arm of service, and Gen Walther asked Napoleon if he could send them to the Mounted Grenadiers of the Guard.) On 26 August the Guard Dragoons had 720 mounted men ready for action, and Gen Arrighi stated that within a month the total would reach 800.

On 21 August 1808, Arrighi's brother Ambroise, a *sous-lieutenant* in the Line dragoons, was killed at Vimeiro in Portugal, in battle against Gen Sir Arthur Wellesley's British landing force; he was the second of the general's brothers to be killed in action.

Napoleon takes command

Junot's corps in Portugal surrendered to the British soon after their defeat at Vimeiro, and by the beginning of winter the British expeditionary corps, now commanded by Gen Sir John Moore, was marching towards Salamanca. For his campaign of reconquest, Napoleon organized his new Armée d'Espagne in six corps, of which II Corps, commanded by Bessières, would be a mixture of Line and Guard units. On 4 November 1808, Napoleon crossed the frontier. Three days later, from Vittoria, he wrote to the empress that more troops were arriving every day, and that he was expecting his Guard shortly (in all, 6,968 Guard infantry and 4,194 Guard cavalry were available to the emperor for this campaign). On 11 November he instructed his ADC Gen Lauriston, who was commanding the Artillery of the Guard, to divide 36 guns between the Guard regiments; six were to go to the Dragoons.

Marching with the emperor was a Vélite of the Dragoons named Jean-Baptiste Fournier, who had left Paris on 16 October (he would

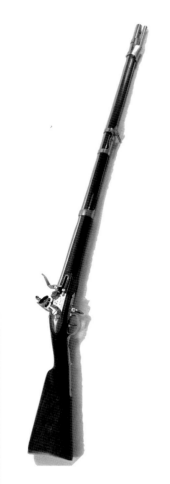

An example of an *An IX*-model (i.e. 1800–1801) musket of fine Guard quality, measuring 142.7cm (56.18in) overall, as issued to the Mounted Grenadiers and Dragoons. This piece was made in 1811; there was no obvious difference between those issued to the two regiments. A shorter, rifled musketoon for the Guard Dragoons is also known. (Musée de l'Empéri, Salon de Provence)

later become Gen Arrighi's personal secretary). In his memoirs he remembered that it took six days to cross the Pyrenees, through overwhelming scenery. Marching through the difficult gorges of Montedragone, on 11 November the army reached Burgos. While the detached commands of Lefebvre, Soult, Lannes, Moncey and Ney defeated several Spanish armies in detail, on 30 November Napoleon arrived before the pass of Somosierra, where he encountered the first serious resistance. The impatient emperor gave the Polish Light Horse of the Guard the order to clear the pass (see MAA 440) – an order they obeyed, at the cost of severe casualties. The Poles were supported by the rest of the Guard Cavalry, and Somosierra would be the first serious action in which the Dragoons took part. With the road to Madrid clear, Napoleon entered the capital on 4 December.

The Dragoons would stay in Madrid for 13 days. With the emperor nearby, the officers always ordered the men to change into their full dress every time that he passed their bivouacs; this caused some frustration, due to the spray of mud thrown up by the rapid passing of the large Imperial entourage.

Napoleon's next target for elimination was Gen Moore's isolated British corps in the north-west, which threatened his lines of communication. The emperor and his Guard left Madrid on 20 December; warned of this on the 23rd, Moore began his painful retreat towards the embarkation ports of Vigo and Corunna. The French pursuit had to cross the snowbound Sierra de Guadarrama, and after the mild weather in Madrid conditions in the mountains came as a shock to Vélite Fournier of the Dragoons.

By night a severe snowstorm transformed the path they were following into an ice rink. Napoleon dismounted and, supported by two Chasseurs of the Guard, made his way downhill on foot. The Mounted Grenadiers were warned in time to retrace their steps, but those still on the crests or on their way up – the Polish Light Horse, Mounted Chasseurs, Dragoons and Artillery of the Guard – were less fortunate, being blocked by drifting snow, or even blown over the edge of the path. Last seen lying beside his horse in a pitiable state, Fournier was reported as missing. After managing to survive the freezing night, he turned back towards the village of Guadarrama. As he descended into the valley his frozen hair came free from the tail of his helmet-crest once more, and his cloak became flexible; it took his horse a dozen sessions of hard shaking to rid itself of the ice-crystals in its coat, mane and tail. It would be some time before Fournier had a chance to take off his boots; when he did, he would discover that his left heel and the side of his foot had been frostbitten. After resting for three hours, Fournier again attempted to cross the pass, and once beyond it he was given a place at their campfire by some Foot Grenadiers of the Guard. Exhausted, he was finally able to rejoin his regiment, who had given him up for dead.

Snow turned into slush and rain as the emperor pushed his men to the limit in order to catch up with the retreating British (and even the Dragoons' regimental dog, which had been with them during the whole campaign, fell victim to the conditions). On 29 December the Mounted Chasseurs caught up with the British cavalry rearguard at the River Ezla crossings near the village of Benavente, where Gen Lefèbvre-Desnoëttes's impetuosity cost him a sharp defeat, many casualties – and his own capture – at the hands of Gen Henry Paget (see MAA 444). The next day Napoleon led the rest of the Guard Cavalry to the river and ordered them across; Fournier saw him, his hat soaked by the rain and his coat covered with mud, pointing out the crossing-places, which were marked by staff officers stationed along the bank. Seeing the Dragoons, he said: 'Dragoons of my Guard, for some time we have been looking for the English; they are on the other riverbank – cross here!'. By fours, with their swords between their teeth and their carbines in their right hands, they entered the water, with the NCOs and officers stationed on the left of the column. Despite the precautions taken, two dragoons and a trumpeter were carried away by the current, but they reached the far bank further down. Once on the other bank the regiment regrouped and took battle formation, but not before most of them had lain down on their backs with their feet in the air, to drain the water out of their heavy boots. Their clothing would stay wet for days before they had a chance to dry it, and frequent snow flurries stuck to the dank cloth. On 6 January 1809 the death of the Dragoons' 1st Lt Meunier was recorded.

1809: THE AUSTRIAN CAMPAIGN

Arriving in Astorga on New Year's Day 1809, Napoleon learned that the Austrian army was mobilizing; for the first time, he had to fight wars on two fronts simultaneously. The emperor left Soult to finish the pursuit of the British (which ended in the failed battle to prevent their embarkation at Corunna), and Lannes besieging Sarragossa; Bessières received the governorship of northern Spain. Napoleon told his brother Joseph that he would be back in 20 or 25 days (in fact, he would never return), and departed. Leaving Bayonne on 19 January, he arrived in Paris early on the 23rd, after covering in less than four days a distance that usually took marching troops three to four weeks.

With his main army in Spain, Napoleon could still fall back on the well-trained forces commanded by Marshal Davout and on those of his German and Polish allies; and his stepson, the Viceroy Eugène de Beauharnais, would bring reinforcements up from Italy. But he needed his Guard back from Spain as soon as possible, and on 15 February he instructed Bessières to send the Foot Grenadiers and Chasseurs, less one battalion from each regiment, back to Paris. The Polish Light Horse, Mounted Grenadiers, Chasseurs and Dragoons were also summoned home, leaving one squadron or two companies from each regiment behind under the command of Maj Chastel.

This fine portrait miniature of a company officer of the regiment shows a uniform differing from regulations (in so far as that term ever applied to officers) only in two respects: the gilt belt buckle bears a raised silver eagle, and there is a line of white piping around the top of the cuff. The sitter is named as 1st Lt 'Charles' Hallé, but the only officer of that surname in the rolls is Robert César Hallé. Born in 1776, he was serving in the 26th Dragoons when he was commissioned first lieutenant in the Guard Dragoons on 21 July 1809. Hallé was awarded the cross of the Legion of Honour in March 1813, and remained with the regiment until its final disbandment on 1 December 1815. (Musée de l'Armée, Paris)

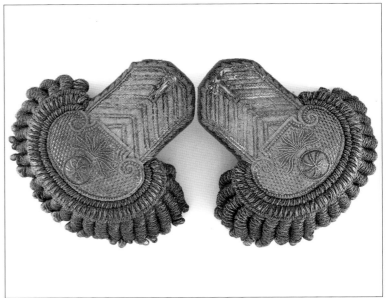

Knowing that the Guard was suffering badly from lack of equipment and clothing, the emperor ordered that the elements staying in Spain should keep the best uniforms, saddles and equipment; but by an order of 9 March, these squadrons too would be called home – Napoleon seemed likely to face 500,000 Austrians with an army of only half that number. On 3 February 1809, the Guard Dragoons who were not serving with the army were recorded as 16 officers with 441 rankers, of which 21 were in hospital and 2 on leave.

Vélite Fournier recounted the march back to France. After several days of preparation the bulk of the regiment, under Maj Letort, left Valladolid on 25 February, but spent a frustrating week halted at San Sebastien. At Bayonne, they learned that the Guard Infantry were to travel by wagon in order to hasten their return, and the cavalry were to march as fast as they could without tiring men and horses excessively. Fournier wrote that they always left at 4am, and usually marched – trotting, or sometimes walking and leading – until 7pm, with frequent stops. They covered between 10 and 12 or more miles per day, depending on the selected overnight quarters. Fournier wrote that the regiment marched as a corps; however, a report from Marshal Berthier to Napoleon stated that one Guard detachment commanded by Gen Lepic had left Bayonne on 15 March with 598 men; on 23 March they were at Bordeaux with 560 Dragoons, and were to be in Paris on 18 April. After arrival at their depot they only stayed for one day in order to draw new uniforms and equipment.

During the night of 21/22 March a Guard detachment consisting of cavalry, artillery, and infantry supply wagons had already left Paris under the command of Gen Arrighi, aiming to reach Metz on 4 April; the Dragoons with this detachment numbered 7 officers and 201 rankers. On 24 March, the Paris depot counted 6 officers of whom 3 were available, 155 rankers and 6 master-craftsmen; 36 troopers were listed as unready for active service, and 25 Vélites were '*non instruit*' – untrained. Of the horses in Paris, 25 were ready to leave; 20 were fit for service in Paris, but not with the army; 45 were under care of the veterinaries, and

69 were too young to serve. Within 24 hours, 20 mounted Dragoons would be ready to leave Paris.

Wagram

On 6 April the Archduke Charles began his invasion of Bavaria, reaching Munich the following day and forcing the king to flee. Napoleon would reassure his ally: 'Within 15 days, you will be back on your throne'. In fact it took only six days, during which the emperor's troops would win six victories, and on 13 May he marched into Vienna.

The Guard were unable to match the emperor's speed. The first of the Dragoons to arrive were those led from Paris by Gen Arrighi; it would be 22 May before the elements led by Maj Letort out of Valladolid on 25 February would arrive at the Abbey of Melk – after marching 2,800km (1,740 miles) in 68 days, with only one-day stops at Paris and Strasbourg. Too late for the victory of Eckmühl (22 April) and the defeat of Aspern/Essling (21–22 May), they found quarters in and around Vienna until ordered to march east, to the island of Lobau at a crossing of the Danube.

On 5 and 6 July, Napoleon crossed the Danube to face the archduke's army at Wagram. The Guard Dragoons and Mounted Grenadiers were kept in reserve, and suffered only from the enemy's artillery fire. One of the casualties was Trumpeter Henry Moulun, aged 22, who had his right arm blown off by a cannonball. (Surviving, he was promoted to trumpet-corporal, and would stay with his regiment – probably at the depot, and for foot service only – until 1 December 1815, when he entered the Hôtel des Invalides.) Another casualty at Wagram was Edmé Nicolas Fiteau, a major in the regiment since 13 September 1806, who had been promoted general to take over the Brigade Lagrange in Gen Count Saint-Sulpice's cuirassier division on 25 May 1809. Wounded at Wagram, he was nevertheless still mentioned as serving with the Guard Dragoons, and it is only on 13 July of that year that we find him as commanding general of the cuirassier brigade. (On 14 December 1810, Gen Fiteau would kill himself while in the grip of insanity.)

Also on 25 May 1809, Gen Arrighi had been commissioned *général de division* commanding 3rd Reserve Cavalry Division, replacing Gen d'Espagne. Major Letort led the Guard Dragoons until 12 July, when Gen Count Saint-Sulpice took over the regimental command. Raymond Gaspard de Bonardi, Compte de Saint-Sulpice, was born in 1761 and active in the army from 1777; a brigade general since March 1803, he was appointed to the Empress Josephine's household in November 1804. He distinguished himself and was wounded at Eylau, and during the 1809 campaign he had taken over Gen Nansouty's 1st Reserve Cavalry Division.

Within days of Wagram, Austria was forced to sue for peace once again. The Guard left for Paris by the end of October 1809, with the intention of reaching the capital in time for the festivities on 2 December that would commemorate the emperor's coronation.

Tail of the Brunon Collection *habit*, showing part of the vertical false pocket indicated by scarlet piping. The scarlet turnbacks are of the style introduced in 1809; they are sewn down permanently, and are cut off square at the bottom – previously the inner points hooked together, leaving a triangle of dark green showing below the junction. Here the grenade ornaments are worked in gold thread on dark green cloth, but this backing was usually white. (Musée de l'Empéri, Salon de Provence)

Trumpeters in parade dress and undress, 1810–14, after Martinet. The mounted man wears the 1810 white *habit* with sky-blue facings edged with gold lace and with gold *brandenbourgs* on the lapels (see Plate F2). The aiguillettes are mixed gold and sky-blue; the helmet plume is sky-blue, but the horsehair *queue* is shown here as black instead of the white one would expect. The man on the right wears a sky-blue *surtout* with scarlet collar, cuffs and turnbacks all edged with gold. The knot of his smallsword is mixed gold and sky-blue, but his aiguillettes are shown entirely gold. (© Collection & photo Bertrand Malvaux, France)

Napoleon could now concentrate on the Peninsula, although, with dynastic problems on his mind, he would not leave Paris himself.[1] On 5 December 1809 he wrote to his minister of war that the Imperial Guard had to be ready to return to Spain, and that Gen Clarke should organize a 1st Guard Division at Chartres on 13 December, commanded by Gen Roguet. The 600-strong cavalry would comprise a squadron each from the Polish Light Horse, the Mounted Chasseurs (plus the Mameluke company), the Dragoons and the Mounted Grenadiers. The men were to be found among those who were in Paris and had not served during the Austrian campaign, and Gen Walther was to assign a major to command this mixed regiment. A 2nd Guard Division, commanded by Gen Dumoustier, would also contain a mixed cavalry regiment, organized in the same way with the exception of the Mamelukes. The emperor would inspect them on 15 December at the Place du Carrousel, and they would leave Paris the next day. A 3rd Guard Division would consist of infantry only, with three guns.

The entire Cavalry of the Guard, plus 60 guns, 4,000 tools and 6 pontoons with a company of pontoneers and Sailors, had to be ready to leave on 1 January 1810. The Guard elements that Marshal Bessières was to lead to Spain would total 19,000 infantry, 4,000 cavalry and 84 guns.

1810–11: ADMINISTRATIVE EVIDENCE

Documents that survive from these years give us indications of the actual strength of the Imperial Guard field forces, and some snapshots of what was actually involved in keeping its units manned and officered even during a period of low-intensity operations. On 25 April 1810, the emperor wrote to Bessières:

> It is my intention to unite in Spain a reserve composed of Guard units. The division of Gen Roguet is already there with 6,000 infantry, 1,200 horses and 8 guns. I will also order the 2nd Guard Division of Gen Dumoustier, which is at Angers, to march towards Burgos. I will also order the Polish Light Horse to head

---

[1] Although his attachment to Josephine was genuine, her failure to provide Napoleon with the heir he craved would lead to his divorcing her in January 1810. In March he married (by proxy) Marie-Louise, daughter of the Emperor of Austria, who would later present him with a son. The regiment's unofficial title was unaffected, and they were prominent in the ceremonies surrounding the second wedding in Paris in April 1810.

for Bayonne, and the Lancers of Berg to march with the Guard. I will give the same order for the 12 light artillery guns which are at Bordeaux. With these forces, I will have in Spain... some 12,000 infantry, the [entire] Polish Light Horse and Berg Lancers, two squadrons of Mounted Chasseurs, two of the Dragoons and two from the Mounted Grenadiers, together with 16 regimental and 12 light artillery guns. This will give a force of 15,000 to 16,000 men.

He also wanted to strengthen the Dragoons, Mounted Chasseurs and Grenadiers by using in Spain those Vélites who had little campaign experience; this would allow him to keep the more experienced soldiers in Paris, and to fill the gaps by means of conscription.

An interesting report of 1810, though lacking an exact date, lists the Guard's forces in Spain, commanded by Gen Dorsenne.[2] The Guard Cavalry Division, commanded by Gen Lepic, had the following strengths:

Regiment	officers	rankers
Mounted Chasseurs	24	365
Dragoons	16	305
Mounted Grenadiers	14	204
Gendarmerie d'Élite	7	103
Polish Light Horse	26	399
Total:	*87*	*1,376*

With the same report, we find a note of the numbers of Vélites who lacked battle experience: with the Mounted Chasseurs there were 120, with the Dragoons 110, and with the Mounted Grenadiers, 46 – in all, 276 Vélites.

Another detailed report, dated 19 September 1810, tells us that the Dragoons in Paris had 61 officers of whom 59 were available for service, 859 rankers of whom 788 available, 34 men in hospital in Paris and 1 officer and 12 men hospitalized elsewhere. In Spain, the regiment had 16 officers and 300 rankers; and 2 officers and 60 men were on leave. The total regimental strength was 80 officers and 1,231 men. The total Guard forces in Spain counted 19,361 officers and men on 19 September; by the end of the year the total was 19,982, of whom 14 officers and 284 men were from the Guard Dragoons. (We also learn that 1st Lt Sub-Aide-Maj Colomier of the regiment was killed in Spain on 5 December 1810, shot in the chest during a reconnaissance.)

Another report showed that no fewer than 579 dragoons were hospitalized during the year 1810, of whom 16 would die, and that 40 were in hospital on 1 January 1811. Nine days later, Gen Count Saint-Sulpice signed the following regimental state: 1,205 men with 1,178 horses, of whom 35 men were to be discharged, and 48 had been selected to pass into the Gendarmerie (such transfers would be a constant factor throughout the regiment's history). This would reduce regimental

---

[2] The strength of the other Guard units and detachments in Spain at this unknown date during 1810 is given as: *Infantry* (divs of Gens Dumoustier & Roguet, 8 regts – 1st & 2nd Tirailleurs-Chasseurs, Tirailleurs-Grenadiers, Conscript-Chasseurs, Conscript-Grenadiers), 296 officers + 11,628 rankers; *Foot Artillery*, 15 + 187; *Horse Artillery*, 12 + 202; *Train*, 13 + 994 (total of 16x 4-pdr & 8x 6-pdr guns, 4x 24-pdr howitzers); *Admin & Medical*, 36 + 370. With the *Cavalry*, listed above, this gives a grand total of 459 officers + 14,757 rankers.

A trumpeter and a dragoon or Vélite in walking-out dress, by Col Jolly. The trumpeter at left wears the 1810 white parade coatee, though Jolly shows the facings as a darker blue; the gold *brandenbourgs* are rather exaggerated, and extend too far down the lapels. The trumpeter carries a smallsword. Despite being in *tenue de ville*, both wear the high, heavy riding boots. (Anne S.K. Brown Military Collection, Brown University, Providence, USA)

strength to 1,122 men and 1,178 horses – a shortfall of 147 men and 87 horses. On 10 March 1811, the Dragoons had 1,178 NCOs and troopers, 91 short of the necessary 1,269; but from those 1,178, one must deduct 52 men who were destined for the Gendarmerie, and 13 who were selected for discharge, so there was still a shortfall of 156 men.

On 19 July 1811, Napoleon asked Marshal Mortier to give him the numbers of Vélites who were not veterans of Wagram; for the Dragoons, Mortier found that there were 125, of whom 41 were serving in Spain. In all, the regiment's detachment in Spain then numbered 14 officers (1 major, 1 squadron-leader, 1 sub-adjutant-major, 1 second lieutenant in charge of food and rations, 1 surgeon-major 2nd Class, 2 captains, 4 first lieutenants and 3 second lieutenants), with 273 NCOs, dragoons and Vélites. The Vélites numbered 46 men, 2 of them former Gendarmes d'Ordonnances.

On 1 August 1811, Napoleon decreed that no more Vélites were to be accepted for the Mounted Grenadiers, Mounted Chasseurs or the Dragoons. All those serving in these regiments on 1 July were retained, but those with less than one year's service or who had not attended the '*école d'escadron*' were not allowed to wear aiguillettes, and could not escort the emperor. The Vélites squadrons would continue to exist until 1 January 1812; on that date they would be disbanded, the men being dispersed into the other squadrons – which would then number five, of 250 men each. On 6 August 1811, Marshal Mortier reported that there were 286 Vélites in the Guard fit to be commissioned as officers, including 25 from the Dragoons.

* * *

The number of reports requested and drawn up suggest that 1810 and 1811 were busy years for the regimental administration. Napoleon was notorious for his appetite for niggling detail (as on 8 August, when the Dragoons had to reply to a request about how many veterans of the Egyptian and first Italian campaigns were still serving – 83 and 34 respectively, and 29 who had fought in both).

Promotions and transfers within the Guard were commonplace. From the Dragoons, transfers to the Gendarmerie were quite frequent. On 19 September 1811, for example, 1st Lt L.A. Crosnier asked for a position as captain in the Gendarmerie. As colonel of the regiment, Gen Count Saint-Sulpice sent his request to Marshal Bessières, who, in his turn, submitted it to the emperor. Crosnier could be replaced within the regiment by 2nd Lt P.A. Desroches, who in his turn could be replaced by SgtMaj L.A. Levasseur. According to the regimental rolls, this request was refused, and Crosnier stayed with the Dragoons until September 1814. (Désroches later became a first lieutenant, but was killed at the battle of Leipzig in 1813, while Levasseur became a lieutenant in the 42nd Line Infantry on 1 April 1812.)

In the pages of the archive we see other men entering and leaving the regiment, like the 20 *élèves trompettes* who joined between 16 October and

1 November 1811; and these mundane records also remind us that a soldier's life was never without risk. On 13 November 1811, for instance, 2nd Lt Landry was wounded on the Vittoria road; and late that December, one Trumpeter Favret got four days in the cells for threatening to beat a cantinière.

In December 1811, Napoleon was looking for a vacancy for a major in the Guard Cavalry, but on the 16th his ADC Count Lobau reported that there were no such vacancies, and indeed that Maj Daumesnil was still serving 'à la suite' in the Mounted Chasseurs, giving that regiment three majors. He went on to suggest that Gen Exelmans might be transferred to the Guard Light Horse Lancer brigade, or to replace Gen Lepic as a major in the Mounted Grenadiers, while Lepic could then command a division of Line cavalry. Another possibility was to replace Gen Letort as a major in the Dragoons, Letort then returning to the Line as a brigade commander.

On 19 December 1811, Bessières send the emperor an overview of Guard Cavalry strength: 4,057 officers and men in Paris, ready to march, and another 1,286 serving in Spain, thus totalling 5,343 all ranks. To fill the establishment, another 403 men with 543 horses were needed. The Dragoons had 826 officers and men, of whom 789 were available in Paris,

51 were in hospital, and 336 serving in Spain, for a total of 1,213 men. This was 136 short of the establishment of 1,349 all ranks. To fill the gaps, the emperor replied two days later that the required men should be found within the 1st–4th and 10th Hussars, and the 10th, 13th–15th, 22nd, 26th, 27th, 29th and 30th Line Chasseurs; each was to provide 10 men from their regimental depots or from those serving in Spain. Additionally, the 20 regiments of dragoons serving in Spain were to provide 10 men each, and the 16 regiments of cuirassiers and carabiniers, 6 men each. The 2nd (Dutch, 'Red') Light Horse Lancers of the Guard were to be brought up to strength with Vélites. In this way, the Guard Cavalry's strength would be increased to about 6,800.

1812: A CAPITAL TOO FAR

Assembly

On 15 December 1811, the emperor asked Marshal Berthier to study the possibilities of withdrawing the personnel – though not yet the horses and equipment – of the Guard units in Spain. His eyes were now turned towards Russia, and increasingly his forces would be moving north and east across Germany as he assembled a Grande Armée of nearly half a million men. Again, the Guard Dragoons' part in this concentration can be traced in part from surviving documents. On 23 January 1812, Guard Cavalry detachments from Paris left Compiègne for Hanover, where they were to receive new horses on 23 February; the largest contingent were 193 officers and men of the Dragoons. In the planned campaign the Guard would fulfil an important role as the reserve, and Napoleon meticulously went through its rolls and inventories. On 27 January, he wrote to Bessières:

> General Saint-Sulpice commands the Dragoons; Col Letort is one of the majors, [but] I do not know the second one – send me a report... I want to place Gen d'Ornano as colonel in one of the cavalry regiments of my Guard. He has always been with the army, and he will acquire self-confidence within the Guard. Later, I will place him with the Line.

To which Bessières replied that 'the second [major] is named Marthod, a fine officer who made his career in the 15th Dragoons, with which he participated in the campaigns of Italy and Egypt. He was considered as one of the finest officers of that regiment.' (Louis Ignace, Baron Marthod had joined the army in 1792, and was a veteran of Arcola and Egypt. Entering the Guard Dragoons as a squadron-leader on 8 July 1807, he was appointed major two years later, with the rank of colonel in the army, and spent most of 1808–11 serving in Spain.)

A month later, Bessières reported that in accordance with the emperor's wishes Guard Cavalry detachments could leave for the army on 2, 3 and 4 March. The first to leave would be 350 Mounted Chasseurs, the next 550 Dragoons, and the third 700 Mounted Grenadiers. This would leave 900 men – 200 Chasseurs, 300 Dragoons and 400 Grenadiers – in Paris; the marshal also stated that he expected about 100 more troopers to arrive at their barracks from hospitals within eight days. Napoleon

Elegant brass helmet '*à la Minerve*' in the former Brunon Collection, worn by the Chevalier Chatry de Lafosse; the associated plume-holder, left, is of later date. Surviving officers' helmets typically show slight differences, some due to contemporary repairs, and some to variations in style – the sweep of the peak was occasionally so pronounced that the wearer must have had to tip his head back to see forwards clearly. (Musée de l'Empéri, Salon de Provence)

instructed Bessières that the detachments were to leave Paris in all secrecy. General Count Saint-Sulpice and Maj Letort of the Dragoons would follow the war squadrons, carrying only one Eagle, and would leave the depot under command of SqnLdr Testot-Ferry.

It is not easy to follow the itineraries of all the Dragoon detachments. Apart from those serving in Spain, those on their way to Hanover or otherwise marching towards Germany, another detachment of 11 officers and 150 men left Paris at 2am during the night of 3/4 March, together with 86 of the 2nd (Dutch) Lancers and 114 Gendarmes d'Èlite; this force commanded by Gen Durosnel was to hunt out recruits who were refusing to join their regiments in the 22nd Military Division. On 9 April 1812, Bessières reported that 300 Mounted Chasseurs, 500 Dragoons, 200 Dutch Lancers and 30 Mounted Grenadiers would leave Paris on the 15th for Mainz, and he also informed the emperor that the Guard Cavalry from Spain had arrived in Paris. They were expected to reach the Rhine on 8 May, the same day that the last detachment would leave Paris.

After steady marching to Dresden, where Napoleon met his allied sovereigns, the Guard crossed the frontier on the River Niemen on 24 June 1812. This next campaign would last until 14 December – five months and three weeks – by which date the Grande Armée would, essentially, have ceased to exist. The Guard, though more sheltered from battle and more disciplined than the Line, would also be reduced to a mere shadow of its former self. After taking so many European capital cities – Berlin, Vienna, Madrid – they had reached out for one capital too far: Moscow.

Eyewitness drawing of a dragoon regiment in battle formation in Russia, 1812, by the German artist Albrecht Adam, who accompanied Prince Eugène de Beauharnais.
(Author's collection)

Until now the Empress's Dragoons had seen action only in minor engagements, and they were hopeful of a chance to prove themselves in a major battle. But except for the Polish and Dutch Lancers, the Guard Cavalry were held in reserve during the march towards Moscow, so suffered only from the heat, bad water, terrible roads and exhaustion. Once in Moscow, Napoleon wrote to Bessières on 15 September that he should organize 20 Dragoon patrols 30 strong, each led by an officer. Divided into four groups of 150 men, they were to occupy the four corners of the city, and clear them of any Russian troops who were still lurking there.

On 25 December, during a reconnaissance near Bourzovo between Moscow and Kaluga, the Dragoons, commanded by Maj Letort, ran into a large force of Cossacks. Confident, and wishing to prove themselves, they charged the enemy – unaware that more Cossacks were waiting for them. Seriously outnumbered, they had to leave dead and wounded on the battlefield, and the recorded officer casualties make it clear that the overall losses must have been high. Among them were SqnLdrs Hoffmayer and Lerivint, Capt Ligier, 1st Lt Pislera and 2nd Lt Hulot, all wounded (Lerivint mortally). Major Marthod and 1st Lt Sub-Adj-Maj Legrand were wounded and taken prisoner; Marthod would die in captivity on 5 November of wounds including a number of lance thrusts, two sabre cuts to his head, and several more to his left shoulder, right arm and left thigh. Major Marthod would be much regretted by the regiment, and Napoleon was furious that a Guard regiment had been decimated by Cossacks.

The retreat

When the emperor's attempts to persuade the Tsar to discuss peace terms failed, he had no option but to retreat towards Poland. On 8 October he ordered that provisions be gathered for the march: for example, biscuits for one month, flour for two, wheat and potatoes for three, and sauerkraut for six months. On 19 October the retreat began; corps after corps left Moscow, shadowed by the ever-present Cossacks. In order to avoid the same route by which they had advanced, Napoleon attempted to head south-west towards Kaluga. The IV and I Corps ran into the Russians at Malojaroslawetz on the 24th; although the French won the battle tactically, Gen Kutusov gained the strategic victory, by forcing the Grande Armée to retreat thereafter directly west through already devastated territory.

The next day, Napoleon and his entourage were halted at Gorodnya when a group of Cossacks suddenly came out of the woods, and at first

were mistaken for French cavalry. When they recognized the danger Murat, Berthier, Bessières and a number of other senior and staff officers drew their swords and gathered around the emperor. The Cossacks repelled the charge of the first, outnumbered Guard escort detachment. Bessières went to look for the other duty squadrons, which always followed the emperor at some distance; returning with those from the Mounted Grenadiers and Dragoons, he succeeded in chasing the enemy off and recovering the guns and carriages they had taken. Major Letort, who was ill, had himself tied into his saddle so that he could charge with the duty squadron. Again, casualties were significant, and among the Dragoons four second lieutenants were wounded – Gandolph (Gandolphi ?), Landry, Leblanc and Lepaumier.

The story of the retreat has been told too often to merit repetition here. Dragging themselves through the snow in the hope of reaching ration depots and shelter first at Smolensk, and then at Wilna (Vilnius), the ranks of the Grande Armée dwindled from starvation, cold, disease, and relentless harrying by their Russian pursuers. On 18 November, 1st Lt Robert of the Guard Dragoons was wounded at Krasnoï; so was Surgeon Aide-Maj de Genssac, who was taken prisoner. The fittest of the infantry and cavalry fought off their pursuers while the army crossed the

Another Albrecht Adam drawing from Russia, showing dragoons in caped riding cloaks amid the grim aftermath of battle. The nearest rider has his musket slung from his saddle. (Author's collection)

engineers' improvised bridges over the Berezina; on 28 November the regiment's 2nd Lt Chabran was wounded there (and would die in the military hospital at Elbing on 28 December). This effort reduced the army's effective strength to about 10,000 men, followed by perhaps twice as many helpless stragglers. At Smorgoni the emperor passed command of the army to Marshal Murat, and left for France on 8 December; just two weeks later he would be at the Tuileries Palace.

Abandoning the army also meant abandoning the Guard, and rivalries led to some generals refusing to obey Murat's orders. The survivors struggled on to Wilna – where some, at least, found food and shelter – and finally to the Niemen frontier crossings. As in other units, large numbers of Guard Dragoons were recorded simply as 'stayed behind' or 'lost'. The Imperial Guard had crossed into Russia 50,000 strong; it reached Wilna with perhaps 2,000 infantry and 800 troopers (though hardly any mounted), the last of them crossing into Poland at Kovno on 13 December. In January 1813, Murat deserted his command and headed back to his Kingdom of Naples, passing his responsibilities to a man of stronger character – Prince Eugène, Viceroy of Italy, who had distinguished himself as commander of IV Corps. In what was probably that admirable officer's finest hour, he gathered up those who still had the strength and will to obey him, and led them back to Germany.

1813: MEN OF BRONZE, AND
MARIE-LOUISES

Rebuilding the Guard Cavalry

Back in Paris, Napoleon had to create, from very limited resources, a new army to hold at bay his increasing numbers of emboldened enemies.

On 30 December 1812 he instructed Berthier to withdraw all unmounted Guard cavalrymen to France, where it would be easier to remount them ('easier' being a relative term – the loss of horses in

(continued on page 33)

COMMANDING OFFICERS
1: General commanding Dragoons of the Guard, court dress
2: *Gén de brigade* Arrighi, 1807
3: *Gén de division* Compte d'Ornano, 1813

F. Courcelle

A

OFFICERS
1: Surgeon 1st Class, *c.*1810–12
2: Junior officer, *grande tenue*, 1808–14
3: Junior officer, *tenue de campagne*, 1806–08

P. Courcelle

B

DRAGOONS
1: *Grande tenue*, 1806–08
2: *Grande tenue*, 1808–14
3: *Sous-officier*,
   non-regulation cloak, 1808–12

F. Courcelle

C

DRAGOONS
1: Dragoon, *tenue de campagne*, pre-1809
2: Brigadier, *petite uniforme*, c.1809–10
3: Dragoon, rear view

F. Courcelle

D

DRAGOONS
1: *Sous-officier, grande tenue, c.*1810
2: Dragoon, summer walking-out dress, *c.*1810
3 & 4: Cloaks and working dress
5: Guard overcoat, 1806–15

F. Courcelle

E

TRUMPETERS & PIONEER
1: Pioneer, *c.*1810
2: Trumpeter, *grande tenue*, 1810–14
3: Trumpeter, service dress, 1806–14

F

TRUMPETER & KETTLE-DRUMMER
1: Trumpeter *grande tenue*, 1806–10
2: Kettle-drummer 1806–10

G

DRAGOONS, *TENUE DE CAMPAGNE*, 1813–15
1: Dragoon, Germany, 1813
2: 2nd Dragoon, Young Guard; France, 1814
3: Dragoon, Belgium, 1815

Russia would remain a chronic handicap during his 1813–14 campaigns). In the meantime, the remnants of the Guard from Russia gathered around Marshal Bessières. His ADC Baudus, who had seen them at Wilna, wrote that compared to the troops of the Line they were still a respectable corps, and other witnesses were also impressed by their majestic air; however few, however gaunt, they were still the Imperial Guard, and still unbeaten by any mortal enemy. (On 7 January 1813, Gen Count Saint-Sulpice wrote instructing SqnLdr Testot-Ferry at the Paris depot to send forward all the uniforms, helmets and sabres that he had, to restore the Dragoons from their miserable appearance.) Soon, these veteran survivors would be considered as an élite within the élite – 'men of bronze' – during some of the Guard's most demanding campaigns.

To fill out the tattered ranks of the Guard Cavalry, the emperor decreed that each of 30 Line cavalry regiments had to pick 10 men who had the required qualities; five of them should have eight years of seniority, the other five only four years. These 300 men would be divided between the Guard Cavalry regiments, and would be considered members of the 'Old Guard'. He planned to organize a light brigade under Gen Colbert of the Red Lancers, composed of the 1st (Polish) and 2nd (Dutch) Lancers, together with the Mounted Chasseurs. The remnant of the short-lived 3rd (Polish) Lancers would join the 1st Lancers, which were still commanded by Gen Krasinski; in Gen Colbert's absence as brigade commander the 2nd Lancers would be led by a major, and the Mounted Chasseurs were led by Maj Lion. All surplus officers were directed to Magdeburg.

Bessières was also ordered to organize a combined regiment of Guard Dragoons and Mounted Grenadiers. One document of 5 January 1813 gave the Guard Dragoons 15 officers in Paris, of whom 11 were available, with 287 rankers, of whom 217 were available. Based on the rolls from the squadrons in the field on 3 December 1812, with the army there were supposedly 64 officers (of whom 3 had been taken prisoner), and 1,020 NCOs and troopers (of whom 15 were in hospital, and 95 had been taken prisoner). The reality was, of course, very different; these 3 December figures dated from a time when the Guard with the Grande Armée was still more or less organized. On 3 January, another document gave the following numbers for men and horses available for the two squadrons of Dragoons that the emperor had ordered organized for the army. The Paris depot had 302 men and 128 horses, of which 218 men and 105 horses were available for service; there was thus a shortfall of 282 men and 395 horses

Portrait of 1st Lt Etienne Nicolas Landry de Saint-Aubin – a striking example of the haughty pride proper to a young officer of the Imperial Guard. The high collars of his shirt and *habit* were very fashionable; and note the strap of his epaulette, covered with protective scales instead of bearing the embroidered grenade badge. Born in Paris in 1780, Landry de Saint-Aubin entered the regiment as a ranker from the 18th Dragoons on 22 June 1806; became a *fourrier* in July 1807; was admitted to the Legion of Honour in May 1808; and was commissioned second lieutenant that August. After the Russian campaign he was promoted first lieutenant on 18 February 1813, and was admitted to the Order of the Reunion (seen here right of the Legion of Honour) in February 1814. Wounded in Spain, Russia and France, he left the army on half-pay on 31 December 1814. (Private collection, France)

from the 500 needed to form two squadrons. Additionally, 300 horses were needed for the survivors of Russia already serving with the army.

Rebuilding the Guard Cavalry required the administrative officers to comb through the ledgers to see what funds were left. Those of the Dragoons were in surprisingly good order, and the controller even advised the minister to congratulate the regimental accountants for saving, over a four-year period, 773,730 francs; on 1 January 1813 the regiment had 1,212,063 francs available – a fortune. (Unsurprisingly, we read that the ministry rewarded them by withholding 57,730 francs that the regiment had been promised to pay their grooms for the years 1807–09, and by immediately freezing, for use elsewhere, all other funds that the ministry was currently due to pay the Dragoons.)

On 11 January 1813, Gen Count Saint-Sulpice was called back to France to become governor of the Palace of Fontainebleau. He would be replaced in command of the regiment by Gen Philippe Antoine, Count d'Ornano – like Gen Arrighi, one of Napoleon's cousins.

Late in January, Marshal Bessières was also recalled to Paris, to organize not just a new Guard but a whole new army. This would have to be built largely from 'Marie-Louises' – new levies of the classes of 1814–15 (so-called because Napoleon's young second empress had to sign the conscription decree in his absence). These new recruits would be less than 20 years old, and most of them had never handled a musket, ridden a horse, or marched long distances; but in just four months they would achieve prodigies while marching beside the veterans in a new Grande Armée. On 29 April 1813 at Weissenfels, where the Marie-Louises faced enemy fire for the first time, Marshal Ney would declare, 'These children are heroes!'.

A decree of 23 January 1813 ordered that a new 300-strong squadron of Guard Dragoons and one of Mounted Grenadiers were to be organized. Of these, 300 men had to be found within the Guard Infantry available in Paris, by choosing those who met the physical requirements and knew at least how to mount a horse; the remaining 300 would be found among the conscripts. They would all be considered as '2nd Dragoons' and '2nd Grenadiers' (Young Guard), paid the same as cuirassiers and dragoons of the Line – though their officers would be Old Guard – and they would form 6th Squadrons. On 15 February, Napoleon ordered that these Young Guard troopers were not to wear aiguillettes, to distinguish them from their brothers-in-arms of the Old Guard. (Later that year they would be absorbed into the other squadrons.)

On 24 January the emperor wrote to Eugène, commanding the Grande Armée at Posen, asking that the 477 Mounted Grenadiers and Dragoons then serving with the army should be organized as one company of each, alongside a squadron of Mounted Chasseurs. The latter, and the combined Grenadiers and Dragoons, were each to be commanded by a squadron-leader, and the whole would be commanded by a major of the Guard. All the rest of the officers, NCOs and men were to be sent back 'en poste'. General Walther was to take his 932 men of the Guard Cavalry from Mainz to Fulda, where all necessary equipment would be gathered. Four squadrons would be organized with these men, and again, all surplus personnel were recalled to Paris (in all, 17 officers of the Guard Dragoons were to return).

In early February 1813 the Dragoons still lacked 521 rankers; 518 men were to be found from the Line cavalry regiments in Spain and selected conscripts. The need for horses was greater; the 945 that were required would be obtained mostly as 'gifts' from the public, and some from a surplus held by the Mounted Chasseurs. On 5 February the Dragoon depot had only 477 complete sets of harness, and the detachment serving with the army only 136 sets; they needed 1,499 harnesses, and of the 886 sets lacking only 400 were promised to arrive by 1 April. Another report of the same date gives us the state of the regiment's six squadrons, not counting the officers:

In France – 513 rankers, of whom 277 available, and 15 on leave or in hospital

In Germany – 469 rankers, of whom 109 available, and 60 on leave or in hospital

This total of 982 NCOs and troopers, of whom only 386 were immediately available, fell far short of the nominal establishment of 1,503 men. The emperor decreed that 700 new recruits were to be raised for the regiment, of whom 182 had to come from within the army, two-thirds of them from the Guard Infantry. As for regimental officers, 15 were serving in France, of whom 10 were available; 57 officers were serving with the army in Germany, though only 11 were immediately available, and 2 were on leave or in hospital. Even the 'paper' strength was thus 21 short of the establishment of 93 officers.

Pierre Alexis (de) Pinteville, colonel of the 30th Dragoons, was commissioned major in the Empress's Dragoons in February 1813, and became a Baron of the Empire that August. While commanding a cavalry brigade at the battle of Toeplitz (17 September 1813) he had part of his face blown away by a shell; thereafter he wore a leather-covered silver prosthesis to hide his disfigurement. Commissioned an honorary *maréchal de camp* (brigade general), he retired in the substantive rank of colonel on 24 January 1815. Nevertheless, in this portrait his dragoon uniform bears the gold embroidery of a general officer. His black lacquered belt, the brass plate unusually embossed with the Imperial eagle, may date from his Line service. (© Musée municipal de Toul, France)

Sabre of an officer of the Guard heavy cavalry, as prescribed for the Mounted Grenadiers, the Dragoons, and (until 1814) the Gendarmerie d'Élite. The blade is partially blued and gilded. Blades for all ranks were made at Klingenthal, but the Versailles factory directed by Boutet was known for the superb finish of its parade and presentation swords for officers – who could, of course, choose whichever source they preferred. (Musée de l'Empéri, Salon de Provence)

On 9 February, Gen Duroc wrote that among the men of the Guard Cavalry regiments in Paris who were available to be sent off to join the army in Germany there were 200 Dragoons with 250 horses. Duroc advised Napoleon to keep enough experienced soldiers in Paris to train the new recruits and to accompany them towards the army (further instruction was routinely given during such marches). The emperor accordingly amended Duroc's figures for this detachment to 100 Dragoons with 200 horses.

Later in February, the squadron of Dragons de la Garde de Paris were ordered to send any of their equipment that might be useful – e.g. helmets, saddlery, etc. – to the barracks of the Imperial Guard Dragoons. (On 18 June the regiment would report that 212 helmets had arrived, but that they were better suited for Line dragoons than for the Guard.)

The Dragoons still lacked 563 men and 800 horses. On 27 February, Napoleon ordered that all Guard troops stationed at Fulda were to march to Gotha, where the Guard would concentrate. On 11 March, Gen Duroc reported the state of the Dragoons as follows: present in Paris – 340, of whom 125 available for the army; on their way to the army – 407; with the army – 334; in hospital, on leave or convalescing – 119; total – 1,200, of the 1,579 needed. In addition, 482 new recruits or replacements out of 927 selected for the Dragoons had arrived at the depot, and others would trickle in as the weeks passed.

On 10 April a more detailed roll of the Dragoons in Germany gave figures for the regiment's depot at Frankfurt-am-Rhine. The commander was Maj Letort, who was assisted by SqnLdrs Testot-Ferry, Clément de Ris and Canevas de St Amand. The total figures do not add up exactly, and seem to include (roughly) the numbers of rankers and mounts represented by a detachment of 3 officers and 100 men with 101 horses under Capt François, which had left Paris on 15 March and was then expected at the Frankfurt depot. On 10 April total strength is given as 25 officers and 729 rankers (of whom 212 were Young Guard '2nd Dragoons'), with 644 horses, organized as follows:

1st Squadron:
1st Company, Capt Ligier – 4 officers, 107 rankers, with 91 horses
7th Co, Capt Bellot – 4 officers, 105 rankers, 90 horses
2nd Squadron:
2nd Co, Capt Sachon – 4 officers, 107 rankers, 91 horses
8th Co, Capt ? – 3 officers, 103 rankers, 90 horses
3rd Squadron:
3rd Co, Capt Raquet – 4 officers, 106 rankers, 91 horses
9th Co, Capt ? – 3 officers, 100 rankers, 101 horses

Another Guard Cavalry detachment, commanded by Maj Lion, which had arrived at Gotha on 26 March, included another 11 Dragoon officers and 115 rankers with 112 horses. These latter soldiers were considered the élite within the élite, and Gen Duroc proposed to disperse them within the companies to stiffen them.

At about this time regimental commanders were allowed to submit nominations for awards of the Legion of Honour. For the Dragoons, 2 squadron-leaders, 1 surgeon-major and 3 captains were proposed for the Officer's Cross, while 3 lieutenants, 1 surgeon 2nd Class, 22 NCOs and 12 dragoons were proposed for the Knight's Cross. Of these 6 Officer's Crosses and 38 Knight's Crosses, Napoleon approved only 3 and 16 respectively.

The German campaign
On 30 April 1813, Napoleon's army assembled 200,000 strong on the Saale river ready to cross into Saxony. The ensuing campaign, remembered in Germany as the Wars of Liberation, would be marked by the steady defection of the emperor's vassals and allies, and would end with the French falling back across the Rhine on 31 October. It fell into two phases: the first lasted from 30 April until 4 June, when the armistice of Poischwitz was signed, and the second from 16 August until 31 October. The Dragoons of the Guard would take a more active part than had been the case in previous campaigns; Napoleon now had no choice but to actually commit his carefully husbanded Imperial Guard as the spine of his army.

At Lützen (2 May) and Bautzen (20–21 May), the emperor won two hard-fought victories over a Russo-Prussian coalition, but was unable to exploit them due to his shortage of cavalry. Napoleon agreed to the Allied request for an armistice that both sides needed, but during this pause Austria took the opportunity to join the Coalition. When hostilities resumed, one of the regiment's casualties was 2nd Lt *porte-étendard* Hebert, wounded near Pirna on 26 August.

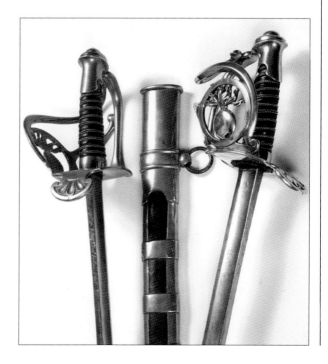

Troopers' sabres of the Guard heavy cavalry regiments, showing the grenade motif incorporated in the bars of the hilt. Between 1808 and 1813 the factories at Klingenthal, Solingen and Versailles produced 4,335 swords of this model. (Musée de l'Empéri, Salon de Provence)

The French won a major victory the following day at Dresden, where 1st Lt Robert was wounded. Dresden would be Napoleon's last serious victory on German soil, because it forced the Allies to reconsider their command structure and strategy. From then on they fought under the general command of the Russian Gen Barclay de Tolly, and adopted a successful strategy of postponing a direct clash with Napoleon in person while they wore down his detached corps in engagements against Marshals Oudinot, Ney and Vandamme. The Empress's Dragoons suffered further casualties, including SqnLdr Raquet (Racquet?), who was killed at Toeplitz on 17 September, and Maj de Pinteville, who had part of his face blown away by an exploding shell in the same battle (see portrait on page 35).

Against this dramatic and bloody background, the more mundane paperwork of the regiment continued to pass back and forth. On 4 August 1813, we find the minister of war asking the emperor what to do with three second lieutenants of the Dragoons named Lepaumier, Hulot and Brabant. During the retreat from Moscow all three had left the ranks to plunder wagons for anything that might help them, and when the unit was rebuilt the regimental administration judged them as unfit for the honour of continued service. They proposed that Lepaumier should be retired due to his infirmities, and that the other two should be transferred to the Line, and so it was decided.[3]

Leipzig and Hanau

Seriously outnumbered, with 195,000 French and allied troops against 430,000 in the converging Coalition armies, Napoleon was finally obliged to face them during the massive three-day battle of Leipzig (16–19 October). On several occasions during these operations the Guard Cavalry charged to save the situation; on 10 October, 1st Lt Decoucy of the Dragoons had already been wounded. During the first day's fighting at Leipzig the Dragoons, commanded by Gen Letort, charged at Wachau, taking a large number of Russian and Austrian prisoners. Among the casualties of Leipzig we find 1st Lt Desroches (Deroches?) killed, and Capt Chamorin and 1st Lt Landry wounded. Unable to break the enemy's lines, and suffering from both shortage of ammunition and the desertion of his German allies, Napoleon was forced to abandon the battlefield and start a retreat to the Rhine – though leaving large garrisons in several German cities and fortresses, where they would remain blockaded.

At Hanau (30–31 October) the Bavarian Gen Wrede attempted to cut off the retreat of what he believed to be a demoralized enemy; in the event, the remnants of the 1813 Grande Armée fought like lions, and none more effectively than the Guard Artillery and Cavalry. They tore through Wrede's blocking force, but at a high cost; in this action the officers of the Dragoons of the Guard suffered more losses than in any other battle. Their wounded were Maj Letort, SqnLdrs Testot-Ferry and Baron Gounio de Saint-Léger, Capt Adj-Maj Barbier, Capts Chamorin and François, 1st Lts Merelle (mortally) and Landry, 2nd Lts Deselve, Carré and Gandolph, and Tpt-Maj Guttmann (Guthmann?) was also hit in the left shoulder.

1814: THE CAMPAIGN OF FRANCE

Early in November 1813 the Grande Armée re-crossed the Rhine at Mainz, reduced by its casualties and detached garrisons to about 80,000 men. For the first time in two decades, the French would be forced to

Philippe Antoine d'Ornano (1784–1863), a cousin of Napoleon's from Ajaccio, Corsica, became a Baron of the Empire in November 1808, and a *général de division* at the age of only 28 in September 1812. He was commissioned colonel of the Dragoons of the Guard on 21 January 1813, and awarded the Grand Cross of the Order of the Reunion – whose breast star and blue riband he wears in this 1814 portrait – on 3 April 1813. After the death of Marshal Bessières on 1 May 1813, d'Ornano commanded the Cavalry of the Guard from 2 May to 29 July. After commanding Guard troops in Paris in 1814, he led the escort that accompanied Napoleon to St Tropez to embark for Elba. Early in June 1815 d'Ornano chose to fight not one but two duels with Gen Bonnet, his consequent wound rendering him unavailable for the Waterloo campaign. He was recorded as 'absent without permission', and was struck from the regiment's rolls. (Musée de l'Armée, Paris)

---

[3] *J.F.L Lepaumier*, b. 1772; Legion of Honour, Sept 1803; entered Dragoons of the Guard as sergeant-major, July 1806; second lieutenant,1807; wounded at Malojaroslawetz, 1812; retired from army 1 Oct 1813.
Antoine Hulot, b. 1770; wounded at Austerlitz, 1805; Legion of Honour, March 1806; entered Dragoons of the Guard as sergeant, July 1806; sergeant-major 1807, second lieutenant 1809; transferred to the Line, 28 Nov 1813.
G.E. Brabant, b. 1772; Legion of Honour, 1806, entered Dragoons of the Guard as sergeant, 26 July 1806; second lieutenant, June 1809; transferred to 28th Line Dragoons, 28 Nov 1813; died of wounds received at Fontenay, 21 March 1814.Their names were not mentioned in the *Almanach Impérial* for the year 1813 (see page 38)

Dragoon of the *Corps royal des Dragons de France*, 1814, by Job after Horace Vernet. This soldier under the First Restoration has a grenade replacing the crown in the corner of the shabraque, which shows only a single *aurore* edging. The helmet has a white Bourbon plume, and a black hair or wool crest. The *fleur-de-lys* visible on the sword belt plate is inaccurate, and, oddly, the aiguillettes are shown on the left shoulder instead of the right. (Collection J.N., France)

fight on their home ground, and there was no time to lose in rebuilding the field army yet again. By New Year's Day 1814 the Allied armies would be crossing France's borders without facing much resistance, and they would soon penetrate deeply into the country.

Napoleon was forced to call again on the troops formerly in Spain, who were now trying to defend the Franco-Spanish border against the Duke of Wellington's British and Spanish invasion army. For the Guard Cavalry, 1,000 Line veterans with four years' service were to be selected, and of these 300 would come to the Dragoons. The emperor even found some troops in Italy, but these needed more time to reach France. More conscripts were levied, but these youngsters would be both sketchily trained and pitifully unprepared for long marches in the bitterly cold winter of 1813/14. (General Colbert would claim that while in the past conscripts had dropped beside the road from exaustion, now they fell out because they were drunk.) New regiments were still organized, such as the three of Scouts of the Guard (see MAA 433); the 2nd Scouts would serve together with the Dragoons and be administered by them.

The Dragoons, both Old Guard and Young Guard, would initially serve in Gen Guyot's division together with the Mounted Chasseurs and Grenadiers; but on 15 March they were transferred into Gen Exelmans' 2nd Guard Cavalry Division, together with 600 men from the Polish Lancers, and 200 Polish Scouts (1st Guard Scouts Regiment). The Dragoons themselves now numbered just 500 men, with another 200 from the 2nd Scouts attached. Before leaving Paris to join the army, on 24 January 1814 Napoleon named Gen Count d'Ornano, colonel of the Dragoons of the Guard, as commander of all the Guard units in Paris.

Strangely enough, the hopeless 1814 campaign would go down in history as one of Napoleon's finest technical achievements. With a usually outnumbered and mostly inexperienced army, he would keep the Allies at bay by a series of rapid marches and counter-marches, beating their separated armies from January until April 1814. The battles of Brienne, Champaubert, Montmirail, Vauchamps and Fère-Champenoise stand as testimony to Napoleon's undiminished skill at manoeuvre, and the bravery of French troops fighting on their own soil.

Among them, the Empress's Dragoons distinguished themselves. At Brienne, they headed the charge of the Guard Cavalry led by Gen Dautancourt, taking three Prussian squares and cutting off their retreat. At Château-Thierry, on 12 February, they would be remembered by brother-officers of the Guard as having made one of the finest charges yet. Inevitably, the cost mounted, as exemplified by the casualties among the Dragoon officers.

At Cohons near Langres, on 13 January, 1st Lt Leblanc and SqnLdr Pictet were wounded (the latter would die of the effects as late as 1 September 1816). Eleven days later, 1st Lt Reiset (Reizet?) was wounded at Bar-sur-Aube. On 12 February, at Château-Thierry, Capt Adj-Maj Barbier, Capts Aguy, Chatry de Lafosse and Dupuy (Dupuis?) were wounded – for some of them, not for the first or even the second time. At Champaubert, on 13 February, Capt Dulac was wounded, and on 5 March, at Rheims, 1st Lt Gilbert (Gibert?). In the bloody battle of Craonne, where the Russian artillery caused havoc, 1st Lt Leblanc was wounded on 6 March, and on the 7th, 1st Lt Landry de Saint-Aubin, 2nd Lt *porte-étendard* Badoureau (Badousseau?), 2nd Lt Sub-Adj-Maj Senet, and 2nd Lts Charpillet and Ponthus, while 2nd Lt Maurio 'stayed behind'. Squadron-Leader Bellot was killed, and 1st Lt Landry and 2nd Lt Giffard were wounded at Laon on 9 March. On 20 March, 1st Lt Landry (yet again) and 2nd Lt Germont were wounded at Arcis-sur-Aube, the latter dying of his wounds on 31 March at Coulommiers.

Actual trooper's sword belt plate worn during the First Restoration, with three *fleurs-de-lys* replacing the eagle on the crowned shield. (© Royal Army Museum, Brussels, Belgium)

With the Guard performing such costly wonders against overwhelming odds, and with most officers already Knights or Officers of the Legion of Honour, Napoleon rewarded several of them on 27 February 1814 with the cross of the Imperial Order of the Reunion. These were SqnLdrs Baron de Gouniou de Saint-Léger and Sachon; Capts Ligier, Barbier, Govon, Chamorin and de Verdière; 1st Lts Landry de Saint-Aubin, Landry and Jomard, and Surgeon-Maj Foucart.

Napoleon's last extraordinary demonstration of his talents finally ended when Paris, neglected, capitulated behind him, and politicians and generals negotiated with the Allied powers. On 11 April 1814 the emperor was forced to abdicate, and departed, with a handful of Guardsmen, for his exile on the tiny Mediterranean island of Elba.

Placed on his throne by the Allies, from May 1814 the restored Bourbon King Louis XVIII organized a Military Household based on the one that had existed before the Revolution; the Imperial Guard lost its predominant position in French society, and even in the army. Although the Bourbons hesitated to disband the Old Guard in order to avoid unrest, their status had to be changed. On 15 May 1814 the king signed the royal ordinance renaming the Old Guard cavalry regiments as the *Corps royal des Cuirassiers de France, des Dragons de France, des Chasseurs à cheval de France* and *des Chevaulégers-lanciers de France*. Each was to be composed of four squadrons, each of two companies, and the Dragoons would number 42 officers and 644 men. Still commanded by Gen Count d'Ornano, the Dragoons – unlike the other regiments – had a white guidon, the traditional shape for dragoons, instead of a standard.

1815: THE HUNDRED DAYS

On 1 March 1815, after escaping from Elba, Napoleon landed on the French coast near Antibes. His progress northwards brought troops flocking to him; Louis XVIII fled, and, without firing a shot, Napoleon returned to the Tuileries Palace on 20 March.

The Dragoons, stationed at Tours, were too far from the scene of these events to play a part, but returned to Paris when summoned by the restored emperor. On 8 April the Imperial Guard was re-created, and the regiment regained their former title, with a stipulated strength of 50 officers and 779 NCOs and troopers; Vélites were also reintroduced. By 30 May, the Dragoons still lacked 100 rankers and 168 horses, but there were 47 surplus *sous-officiers* and *brigadiers* (sergeants and corporals) on the rolls. The emperor told Gen Drouot to keep these NCOs in the ranks fighting as troopers for the time being, and to buy horses using some of the 4 million francs he had been given. The regiment was now to number 1,000 men in four squadrons – 800 veterans and 200 Vélites – and when they went on campaign they were to leave 48 veterans and 50 Vélites at their depot.

The same decree announced that the Mounted Grenadiers, Mounted Chasseurs and Dragoons were each to be divided into two *régiments de marche* of two squadrons, each element being commanded by a major, both coming under a single administration and the supervision of the colonel of the regiment. The Dragoons' colonel, Gen Count d'Ornano, was not destined to take the field in June 1815. On the 7th of that month he and a Gen Bonnet fought a duel, each firing three pistol shots with no result whatever. The following day they met again, and this time both men were wounded. General Letort, now an ADC to the emperor, took over command of the regiment, assisted by Maj Hoffmayer.[4]

On 1 June 1815 the regiment numbered a staff of 12 men, and four squadrons, with 63 officers and 910 men. The 1st Sqn listed 225 men; the 2nd, 226; the 3rd, 224, and the 4th Sqn, 223 men.

Before dawn on 15 June the French army crossed the Belgian border and marched towards Charleroi; the Dragoons and Mounted Grenadiers made up Gen Guyot's 2nd Guard Cavalry Division. At 4pm, learning that the advance had slowed down near Gilly, Napoleon went to see for himself, taking his ADC Gen Letort; once on the spot the emperor brusquely settled an argument between Marshal Grouchy and Gen Vandamme, ordering Vandamme to advance. Seeing Prussian troops retreating in good order, Napoleon ordered Gen Letort to charge them with the four Guard duty squadrons, of which one was from the Dragoons. Letort's charge was successful, even overrunning a few hastily-organized squares; but he himself was shot, and would die two days later, so command of the regiment passed to Maj Hoffmayer.

It was he who charged with them at Waterloo on 18 June. The wider story of that epic defeat does not need repeating here. General Guyot led at least three charges against the Allied squares, and had two horses killed under him before being forced by his wounds to leave the field; his replacement, Gen Jamin, was killed only moments later. Officer casualties among the Dragoons of the Guard were: at Ligny on 16 June, Capt Tiercé killed; wounded at Waterloo, SqnLdr François, Capt Leblanc (Young Guard), and Capt Herissant (died of wounds in Charleroi, 26 June); 1st Lts Bourlier, Degascq, and Lapierre (died in Brussels, 15 July); 2nd Lts Bellehure, Monneret, d'Hebrard, and Poulain (died in Paris, 3 July).

After Napoleon's second abdication the Guard units were ordered to withdraw southwards behind the River Loire, and all would be disbanded within a few months. For the Empress's Dragoons, the last trumpet sounded on 1 December 1815.

General Louis Michel, Count Letort (1773–1815); again, note the shirt collar worn fashionably high. Normally a white cravat was worn over the shirt and under the coatee collar in peacetime, and a black one in wartime. Joining the regiment as a major from the 14th Dragoons in November 1806, Letort was created a Baron of the Empire in 1810. He distinguished himself at Gorodnya on 24 October 1812, and at Viazma on 3 November; promoted *général de brigade* in January 1813, he continued to serve as a major with the regiment, distinguishing himself yet again at Wachau on 16 October, and being wounded at Hanau on 30 October. Promoted *général de division*, he led the Old Guard Cavalry Division in early 1814 until the arrival of Gen Lefèbvre-Desnoëttes. He rallied to Napoleon during the Hundred Days, and died of wounds on 17/18 June 1815.

---

4 Laurent Hoffmayer, b. Sept 1768 in German principality of Fürstemberg; commissioned captain in 29th Dragoons, 1803; Legion of Honour, 1806; entered Dragoons of the Guard as captain, 8 July 1807; colonel of 2nd Dragoons, Feb 1813. As Baron of the Empire and Officer in the Legion of Honour, on paper became a major in 2nd Scouts of the Guard – the regiment attached to the Empress's Dragoons – but is stated never actually to have left the latter. During First Restoration stayed with *Corps royal des Dragons de France*, passing into Dragoons of the Guard during the Hundred Days; retired on half-pay, 16 December 1815.

PLATE COMMENTARIES

In a period when clothes were a visible sign of social status, among the privileges enjoyed by the Imperial Guard were uniforms made of superior quality materials than those for the Line. The cut of the Dragoons' uniform followed that of the Mounted Grenadiers; the coats were of a darker green than found elsewhere in the rank-and-file of the army, and officers adopted even darker shades for their privately tailored coats. While a more ordinary model of dragoon helmet may have been used briefly before the appearance of the famous 'casque à la Minerve' (see Plate C1), the latter seems to have been basically unchanged from 1806 to 1815 – though every single surviving example shows some subtle variation.

A: COMMANDING OFFICERS

A1: General commanding Dragoons of the Guard, court dress

This might be GenDiv Louis Michel, Compte Letort, the last commanding officer of the regiment, who was mortally wounded during the Waterloo campaign. The interest of this rear view lies in the relative simplicity of the coat, with the general officer's embroidered gold oakleaves only on the collar, the turnbacks, and around the waist buttons.

A2: Général de brigade Louis Arrighi de Casanova, 1807

Known for his personal courage, this cousin of Napoleon was wounded at Salahieh in 1798 during the Egyptian campaign; commissioned captain on the battlefield, he was again wounded near Saint-Jean d'Acre, and was rewarded with a 'sabre of honour' and appointment as an ADC to Gen Berthier. He distinguished himself at Marengo, and served from 1801 with the 1st Dragoons, becoming *chef de brigade* (colonel) in August 1803. At Austerlitz in 1805 he commanded the 9th Dragoons, a fashionable Parisian regiment, and the following year was appointed, at the age of 28, the first colonel of the Dragoons of the Guard, despite not being a general officer until June 1807. Note the senior officers' *aigrette* plume of white heron feathers; the gold-and-blue waist sash of brigade general's rank, and the double holster-covers on his saddle, both of which date the figure to 1807. Arrighi was named a commander of the Legion of Honour in 1804, but biographies (strangely) do not mention any higher decorations.

A3: Général de division Philippe Antoine, Compte d'Ornano, 1813

Another of Napoleon's cousins, Gen d'Ornano became colonel of the regiment on 21 January 1813, but in fact spent only a few months with it. This shows him in the magnificent uniform that can be admired today at the Musée de l'Empéri in Salon de Provence; note the gold general officer's embroidery on the collar of his regimental coat, and the gold-and-red sash of his army rank. His breast star, and the diagonal light blue riband, are those of the Grand Cross of the Order of the Reunion. The crimson shabraque bears a gold imperial crown and is trimmed with gold, as are the triple covers on the saddle holsters, which replaced double covers from 1808–09.

B: OFFICERS

B1: Surgeon 1st Class, c.1810–12

Based on that of Surgeon Foucart, now at Les Invalides in Paris, the coat is in regimental green with scarlet lining, but has collar, lapels and cuffs in crimson velvet. Surgeons displayed gold foliate loops on the collar and cuffs; loops on the breast and pockets distinguished surgeons 1st Class. The aiguillettes identify him as a member of the Guard, but since he is not a military officer he wears no epaulettes – the gold trefoil shoulder knots are purely decorative. We have given him nankeen breeches – *nankin*, a light buff cotton – for summer dress, and hussar-type boots 'à la Souvarov', though he might equally wear dark green breeches and the higher, rigid 'butcher' boots.

B2: Junior officer, *grande tenue*, 1808–14

The classic silhouette of an officer in full dress, after Martinet. Determined that his new regiment should look both elegant and modern, the young Col Arrighi shortened the coat-tails, and abolished kneebreeches, stockings, buckled shoes, and queued and powdered hair. The conservative Marshal Bessières, colonel-general of the Guard Cavalry, was scandalized, but as a cousin to the emperor Arrighi enjoyed great latitude regarding uniforms.

The regimental dark green *habit* coatee has white lapels, but his gauntlets hide the scarlet cuffs and white cuff patches. The coat is steeply cut away at the front, revealing the white waistcoat. Note the large scarlet feather plume on the 'Minerva' helmet; the gold fringed epaulette on the left shoulder only for company officers, balanced by a fringeless *contre-epaulette* and the Guard aiguillettes on the right; and the scarlet false-pocket piping, lining and turnbacks, the latter with gold-thread flaming grenade ornaments worked on white backing. The triple holster covers and the shabraque are edged with one broad gold stripe between two narrow, within a red outer piping; this may date the figure to 1813–14.

B3: Junior officer, *tenue de campagne*, 1806–08

Reconstructed from period documents, this officer in the field wears a typical single-breasted *surtout* for everyday use, to save wear-and-tear on his expensive full-dress coat. He displays the ribbon of the Legion of Honour on his left breast, apparently attached with a gilt pin – such details were matters of individual taste.

C: DRAGOONS

C1: Dragoon, *grande tenue*, 1806–08

The 'broken' profile of the helmet, which may indicate a so-called 'movable peak' (i.e. the peak made as a separate piece, then attached), is closer to a Line dragoon headpiece than a 'Minerva'. The two holster covers date this figure earlier than 1808–09, perhaps supporting the idea of an early issue of such helmets. The green *habit* of the rankers bore two *contre-epaulettes* and right-shoulder aiguillettes in the pinkish-orange shade called *aurore*, and the turnback ornaments were *aurore* grenades on white backing. Deerskin breeches of a yellowish buff colour were worn for full dress in attendance on the emperor, and breeches of shaven sheep's-hide for other duties. The horse furniture was green with *aurore* trim – single narrow and broad stripes, with a red outside-edge piping. The sword belt at the waist supports the same type of sabre as carried by the Mounted Grenadiers of the Guard, and a bayonet; the pouch belt is worn over the left shoulder (see Plate D3 for these details). The musket, supported by a strap loop and a butt 'bucket' from the saddle, is the 1777 dragoon model modified in *An IX* or *An XI*, and two *An IX* pistols were carried in the saddle holsters. A typical ammunition issue was 30 cartridges.

C2 : Dragoon, *grande tenue*, 1808–14

This figure is reconstructed from regulations and contemporary items. The helmet is the one-piece 'Minerva' pattern, with a sweeping front profile almost continuous from the peak to the foot of the crest. It is of *cuivre jaune* (brass), the peak and lower skull covered with an unshaven hide 'turban' coloured to resemble leopardskin. A black horsehair tail (*queue*) passes inside the hollow brass crest, with a stiff bunch of hair emerging from a *porte-aigrette* at the front top, and the falling tail emerging at the back (see Plate D3). The front of the crest is embossed with a grenade and a crowned Imperial eagle. All junior officers and rankers wore a scarlet feather plume from a holder on the left side, in front of the star boss of the brass chin scales. The coat, the buff hide riding breeches, and the semi-rigid *bottes demi-molles* are as C1. The latter have stiff knee-pieces stitched to softer leather legs

The uniform of Gen d'Ornano (see Plate A3) bears three types of buttons: the 1803 Republican 'RF' type; the 'EF' of the Empire; and the Guard eagle button of the Hundred Days – during the First Restoration he presumably wore a fourth type, the three-lily buttons of the Bourbons. Rather plain for a divisional general, the coatee lacks gold oakleaf embroidery on the lapels or cuffs, bearing it only as on Plate A1. The lapels and cuff patches are elegantly tailored in a pronounced scalloped shape; note also the short tails, by comparison with the sleeves. (Musée de l'Empéri, Salon de Provence)

(compare with the officers' heavier one-piece 'butcher boots' on Plates A & B). Pictorial evidence suggests that the musket, and therefore the bayonet, were laid aside for mounted duty late in the Empire, but it is difficult to know exactly when; certainly, an instruction of 1 December 1812 specified that the regiment's master-saddler should make up 1,000 black leather lock-covers for muskets. Note, strapped on top of the portmanteau, the riding cloak folded to show its scarlet lining.

C3: *Sous-officier* in non-regulation riding cloak, 1808–12

'Regulation' was a comparative term in the Imperial Guard, where orders on such matters as secondary clothing were probably often verbal only, especially for higher ranks. While there is no documentary evidence, some sources suggest that senior NCOs wore this dark green caped *manteau trois-quarts*, recalling a type worn by officers, instead of the rankers' issue type in grey-white cloth (see Plate E3). All such garments were lined scarlet at the front and inside the rear vent. Note the helmet plume wrapped in protective oilskin; in the field in dirty weather it was often removed and packed away for safety.

D: DRAGOONS

D1: Dragoon, *tenue de campagne*, pre-1809

This figure is from a document known as the Otto de Bade Manuscript, which can be dated to about 1807. It shows a helmet with a more 'broken' front profile, as discussed under C1. For everyday wear this dragoon wears a regulation green single-breasted *surtout*, with nine front buttons, and (hidden here) plain green cuffs. It is otherwise identical to the full-dress *habit*. The original illustration shows no bayonet

The maker's label on the scarlet backing of the *contre-epaulette* of a squadron-leader of the regiment (worn on the left by this rank). An amendment dates it to the First Restoration: 'HEBERT, / POUPARD et JARRE, / Passementiers [roughly, costume trimmers] de la / GARDE IMPÉRIALE, / Rue S-Sauveur No.14, / À PARIS' – but the word 'Impériale' has been neatly crossed out. By comparing promotion dates, we can deduce that these epaulettes belonged to the Chevalier Chatry de Lafosse, owner of the helmet shown on page 21, who attained the rank of *chef d'escadrons* in March 1814. (© Collection & photo Bertrand Malvaux, France)

being carried. The lighter green shade shown for the horse furniture probably represents the appearance of coarser material than that of the uniform.

D2: Brigadier, petite uniforme, c.1809–10
Corporal's rank was marked by two diagonal stripes of *aurore* woollen lace on both forearms. From about 1809 the single-breasted *surtout* began to be replaced for everyday dress with this *habit de petite uniforme* (confusingly, this was also sometimes termed a *surtout*). It resembled the full-dress *habit* in all respects except for plain green two-button cuffs, and was apparently made of cheaper materials or from worn-out full-dress coats. The sword belt, of stitched, whitened 'buff'-leather of Guard quality, could be worn either around the waist or diagonally from right shoulder to left hip; its brass plate bore an eagle on a shield beneath a crown.

D3: Dragoon, rear view
Seen from this angle, the soldier might equally be wearing either the *habits* of full dress or *petite uniforme*, or even a single-breasted *surtout*. Note the two falls of horsetail emerging from the sides of the helmet crest quite high up; at a later date it would be a single fall, emerging at the bottom of the crest. The *aurore* woollen chevron on the upper left sleeve marked four years' service – a very common distinction among men of the Imperial Guard. Note the details of the sabre, and of the pouch belt; the pouch flap bore a brass lozenge stamped with the same device as the sword-belt plate.

E: DRAGOONS

E1: Sous-officier, grande tenue, c.1810
This sergeant-major, reconstructed from the regulations, wears the same uniform as the rank-and-file, but privately

tailored of better materials, as was very common for those who could afford it. He is distinguished by shoulder ornaments – including a left epaulette – of mixed red wool and gold lace. The same colours are seen in his two diagonal sleeve-stripes of rank, and his sword knot. Sergeants and above did not carry the musket and bayonet.

E2: Dragoon in summer walking-out dress, c.1810
This figure, after a sketch by Martinet, shows why the elegant Dragoons of the Guard were nicknamed '*les Muscardins*', a slang term for French Revolutionary dandies. The plain black bicorne prescribed for *tenue de ville* displays a tricolour cockade held by an *aurore* lace loop from a uniform button. Its shape is fashionable – as is the high white shirt collar, lifted above the coat collar. The short gloves reveal the scarlet cuffs and white cuff patches of the *habit*. The shade of breeches shown by Martinet suggests nankeen, worn in hot weather instead of dark green woollen cloth. They have been interpreted elsewhere as the deerskin breeches, but these were reserved only for full-dress wear by those in close personal attendance upon the emperor. The sword belt is worn over the right shoulder, revealing one of the two rings uniting its three sections; a hook further back allowed the sabre to be hitched up by its upper scabbard ring, but for walking-out it was carried under the arm.

E3 & E4: Dragoons in working dress
They are riding out bareback on a cold morning, perhaps to gather forage or firewood. Both wear the regimental *bonnet de police* (see photograph on opposite page), the dark green single-breasted stable jacket, and grey buttoned overalls over shoes. E3, reconstructed from regulations, shows the *manteau-trois quarts*; this voluminous riding cloak was made of white cloth with interwoven blue threads, partially lined with scarlet, and had a green collar. E4, from regulations and a contemporary engraving, shows the post-1813 *manteau-capote*; this had a plain collar, sleeves, and fringed *aurore* lace '*brandenbourgs*' from the three buttons of the cape.

E5: Dragoon in Guard overcoat, 1806–15
This figure follows Lucien Rousselot's reconstruction from the regimental accounts. It suggests the existence of a sleeved, caped watchcoat (note the deep sleeve turnbacks) that anticipated the general-issue 1813 *manteau-capote*. This accords with Col Arrighi's demand that his men be issued with such garments at Metz during a foot march in December 1806. A detachment that left Paris on 13 November to join the field army were equipped with cloaks and high cavalry boots – highly unsuitable for dismounted marching in severe weather – and many suffered from frostbite or fell sick. Colonel Arrighi was furious, and when he asked for long overcoats Gen Dejean refused them. Confident in his status as a kinsman of the emperor, the young colonel wrote directly to the Arch-Chancellor of the Empire, Cambacérès, insisting that his men should receive long coats when they arrived in Metz on 26 December; he also wrote to Napoleon. Dejean was reprimanded, and the Guard Dragoons got their coats.

F: TRUMPETERS & PIONEER

F1: Pioneer, c.1810
This figure is taken from the only known source for a pioneer of the Dragoons of the Guard, the early and generally respected 'Alsatian Collection'. Research by Lucien

Rousselot failed to locate in the regimental accounts any mention of pioneer equipment, but we do not believe that the absence of paperwork is definite proof that such items did not exist – the Guard was often a law unto itself in matters of uniform, and pioneers would seem to be a necessary component of the *tête-de-colonne* of a dragoon regiment. The bearskin is dressed with *aurore* cords, tassels and flounder as well as the regiment's scarlet plume, and a grenade over crossed axes in *aurore* appears on both upper sleeves. The soft leather apron is configured in such a way as to be practical for wear on horseback.

F2: Trumpeter, *grande tenue*, 1810–14

This figure is reconstructed from regimental accounts and period iconography; it can be dated by the fact that there is no evidence for trumpet-banners (*tabliers de trompette*) before 1810. This white uniform faced with sky-blue and lavishly trimmed with gold lace was often painted, but probably rarely worn; it was kept in barracks, and only authorized for exceptional occasions, e.g. for parades attended by the Empress Marie-Louise. Clearly, it was very expensive and easily soiled, and we know that it was difficult to clean. The woollen material could not be washed, so it had to be simply beaten to remove dust, and any stains needed careful cleaning. The horse furniture is in matching sky-blue with gold trim.

F3: Trumpeter in everyday service dress, 1806–14

Reconstructed from the regimental accounts, this figure shows the gold-trimmed dark sky-blue *surtout* (a colour supposedly chosen by the Empress Josephine herself), which was worn for everyday duties both in barracks and in the field. Martinet shows a variation with scarlet collar and cuffs (see page 16). Note that while the horse furniture is sky-blue it is trimmed with *aurore*, more practical for daily use than expensive gold lace.

G: TRUMPETER & KETTLE-DRUMMER

G1: Trumpeter, *grande tenue*, 1806–10

The sky-blue *habit* with white lapels and gold lace trim was worn for full dress even after the introduction of the white version shown as F2; it is dated here to 1810 at the latest only by the absence of a trumpet-banner.

G2: Kettle-drummer, 1806–10

This figure, following Lucien Rousselot after the contemporary Alsatian Collection, shows a black drummer, although only the names of three French drummers are recorded. (We should recall that the regiment's patroness, the Empress Josephine, was a white Creole from Martinique.) The relatively simple oriental costume accords with practice pre-1810. From that year, when Napoleon's wedding to Marie-Louise in April saw the introduction of several new ceremonial uniforms for Guard Cavalry regiments, a much more elaborate version was certainly adopted, but unfortunately evidence for it remains undiscovered.

Background: For the dismounted

guard duties performed at times by all cavalrymen, the Dragoons wore shoes and white gaiters in place of boots, and their sword belts from right shoulder to left hip with the sabre hooked up.

H: DRAGOONS, *TENUE DE CAMPAGNE*, 1813–15

H1: Dragoon, Germany, 1813

This figure is taken from a painting of the battle of Hanau by Horace Vernet, an official artist known for his well-documented and precise studies of troops. Under the late Empire new helmets were made with a small rear peak to protect the back of the neck, and from 1813 they had a Medusa's head above the shield on the front of the crest. Note the absence of a musket. The horse furniture has *aurore* trim in one broad between two narrow stripes – a pattern that does not conform to any known documentation.

H2: 2nd Dragoon of Young Guard; France, 1814

By regulation, this young dragoon rides to war wearing the simplified coatee of *petite uniforme* (see D2), and breeches of coarse grey woollen cloth. He does not wear the distinguishing aiguillettes of the Old Guard, and his helmet will never receive the regiment's red feather plume. Although the triple holster covers are shown here, it is possible that for reasons of economy they were not issued to the Young Guard squadrons.

H3: Dragoon, Belgium, 1815

In May 1815, factories were established to turn out 500 new Guard uniforms per day, but in fact – contrary to popular legend – during the Hundred Days most Guard units, for lack of funds, were less well uniformed and equipped than those of the Line. The Guard Dragoons were an exception, however. A year previously they had passed directly into Bourbon service; few changes to their existing uniforms had been ordered (see the painting by Job on page 40) – and to what extent these unpopular alterations were actually made is uncertain. The shield on the front surface of the helmet crest was supposed to display three *fleurs-de-lys* instead of the eagle. We show this dragoon at Gilly or Waterloo still ostensibly in his old Imperial uniform, though without a helmet plume. His grey-brown overalls are Line heavy cavalry issue; he carries no musket, and has his riding overcoat rolled and tied around his body.

Fatigue cap – *bonnet de police* – of a ranker in the Empress's Dragoons (see Plates E3 & E4). The 'flame' and 'turban' are dark green, the former piped and tasselled with *aurore*, the latter with broad woollen lace of the same colour. Two slight variations are known. The first type, pre-1812, had the grenade badge worked in *aurore* on dark green cloth, and dark green edge-piping to the turban. This is the second type, introduced during 1812, with white backing to the grenade, and white edge-piping to the turban. (© Collection & photo Bertrand Malvaux, France)

INDEX

References to illustrations are shown in **bold**.
Plates are shown with page and caption locators in brackets.